MAKING
DECORATIVE
BOXES

MAKING DECORATIVE BOXES

Cheryl Owen

David & Charles

A DAVID & CHARLES BOOK

First published in the UK in 2002
by David & Charles
ISBN 0 7153 1222 7 (hardback)

Distributed in North America
by F&W Publications, Inc.
4700 E. Galbraith Rd.
Cincinnati, OH 45236
1-800-289-0963
ISBN 0 7153 1451 3 (paperback)

executive art editor **Ali Myer**
desk editor **Jennifer Proverbs**
text editor **Jo Richardson**
designer **Jane Lanaway**
photography **Ginette Chapman**
production controller **Jennifer Campbell**

Printed in Italy
for David & Charles
Brunel House, Newton Abbot, Devon

contents

introduction

CANISTER, CASKET AND CHEST; square, round and oval; large, medium and miniature. Think of boxes, in all their variety of forms, beyond their everyday, mundane storage function and see them instead as unique vehicles for display, customized containers for special gifts or protectors and preservers of precious keepsakes. And of course, a beautifully handcrafted box is a treasured gift in its own right.

Boxes offer endless scope for creative craftwork, whether in making the containers themselves or decorating them – it's a great way to try out a new craft or experiment with different materials. Since only small amounts of materials are needed to make or transform even the largest container, you may discover that you have an inspiring yet inexpensive source to hand – left-over paint and wallpaper, oddments of giftwrap and fabric, ribbons, beads and buttons.

The following pages present detailed techniques and innovative schemes for both revamping old or plain boxes and crafting them from scratch in a range of materials, from traditional card to contemporary wire and clay. Grouped according to medium, the easy-to-follow projects are accompanied by trace-off templates to ensure a professional result. To help you create your own, alternative designs, there are suggestions for variations as well as additional motifs or patterns. Also included are inspirational and practical ideas for presenting and using the finished items.

tools and equipment

Most of the projects in this book use basic craft equipment that you may already possess. For comfort and safety, work on a clean, flat surface that is well lit and remember to keep sharp tools, glues and paint away from children and pets. Old plastic carrier bags cut open and laid flat provide water-resistant protection to the surface underneath when working with clay and paints.

drawing tools

Use HB pencils for drawing. Keep them sharpened to a point or use a propelling pencil. Use a ruler and set square when drawing squares and rectangles so that the lines are straight and the angles accurate. Draw circles with a pair of compasses. An air-erasable pen is recommended for drawing on fabric, since the ink will gradually fade away – always test on scrap fabric first.

cutting tools

Sharp scissors are vital for craftwork. Use small, pointed needlework scissors for intricate work. Use dressmaking scissors to cut fabric but not to cut paper, since it will blunt the blades. Pinking shears will prevent fabric from fraying and will also give a decorative zigzag edge to the cut.

Craft knives give a neat cut to paper and card and are best for cutting card. Always use a craft knife on a cutting mat. Plastic cutting mats are available from art and stationery shops and suppliers. The surface is self-healing so can be used continually and is slower to blunt blades than other surfaces. Alternatively, improvise by cutting on a sheet of thick card. Remember to change blades regularly, since a blunt blade will tear paper and card. Cut straight edges against a metal ruler.

Use metal cutters or an old pair of scissors to cut fine metal and wire cutters to cut wire. Bend wire with pliers. Use a bradawl or an awl to pierce holes through card and to prepare a hole in wood for drilling.

adhesives

Always follow the adhesive manufacturer's instructions clearly and test it first on any scraps. Use a plastic spreader to distribute the glue evenly or improvise by using a strip of card. A cocktail stick or toothpick is useful for applying tiny amounts of glue.

All-purpose household glue will stick paper, card, fabric, ribbon and lightweight craft materials. Fabric glue, which is usually latex, will stick fabrics, ribbons and threads. PVA (polyvinyl acetate) is a very versatile, inexpensive adhesive. It is a white, non-toxic adhesive that dries to a clear finish and will stick card, fabric and mosaics. Alternatively, use any white glue.

Spray glues give an even coat of adhesive and are ideal for use on large areas. Use spray mount adhesive to stick paper, lightweight card and lightweight fabrics. Use art and hobby spray adhesive on heavyweight cards and fabrics. Always test spray adhesives on scraps of fabric first, since the glue may seep through to the right side. Protect the surrounding area with scrap paper or newspaper and spray in a well-ventilated room.

Gummed paper tape is an inexpensive traditional tape, usually brown in colour, used to construct boxes. Simply moisten the tape to make it sticky. Double-sided tape is a clean, neat way to join layers together and can be used on paper, card and some fabrics. Masking tape is very useful for sticking work temporarily in position. Use low-tack masking tape and check first that it will not tear or mark the work.

This small range of basic craft equipment is all you will need to create most of the decorative boxes throughout the book.

basic tool kit

Many of the following items are used in every project and are therefore not listed in the materials and equipment lists, so make sure that you assemble this basic kit before you begin any project.

pen	tracing paper (for making templates)
sharp pencil	PVA or white glue
metal ruler	all-purpose household glue
craft knife	
cutting mat	spray mount adhesive
sharp pair of scissors	art and hobby spray adhesive
pair of compasses	
double-sided tape	masking tape

painting tools

Good-quality artist's paintbrushes are worth the expense and they will last a long time if cleaned and looked after properly. Use a fine brush for detailed work. Flat paintbrushes are useful for giving an even coverage of paint. A stencil brush is good for applying paint in a dabbing motion. A natural sponge can be used to apply paint for a random effect or use an old toothbrush to spatter paint. Painting stamps can be made from Neoprene foam glued to corrugated card. Always clean painting tools immediately after use.

modelling equipment

Store clay that is not in use in an airtight container. Roll clay out flat with a rolling pin and cut it with a small kitchen knife. Use a cocktail stick or toothpick and specialist modelling tools for shaping the clay. Roll and model the clay on a cutting mat, bread board or greaseproof paper.

materials

choosing boxes

Both the type of decoration that the box will have and its use affect the choice of material for making the box. Boxes are mostly constructed of card, wood or metal, but glass boxes and those woven from rattan and similar materials are also available. It's also easy to make boxes from clay, as you will see in some of the projects.

CARD Boxes made from card should have lightweight decoration, or be covered in paper or fabric, or painted. Choose the paints carefully, since some paints will warp the card. Heavy objects should not be stored in card boxes but are ideal as hat boxes, gift boxes and for display. It's simple to make your own boxes to your personal specifications. Craft shops sell card box 'blanks' ready for embellishment, and shoe boxes can be given a new life just by covering them in giftwrap or fabric. Add a metal label holder to the front and they make smart containers for stationery and computer disks.

WOOD Wooden boxes are more versatile and can take weighty applications of, for example, mosaics and pebbles. Specialist mail-order companies supply wooden box 'blanks' in a variety of sizes, from tiny jewellery caskets to blanket chests (see Suppliers, page 112). Look out for interesting boxes to revamp at junk shops. Second-hand wooden boxes may need some preparation first. Fill any cracks with wood filler, and sand uneven or poorly painted or varnished surfaces. Wooden boxes without lids, such as seed boxes, can be turned into characterful containers for plants.

METAL Paint metal boxes with spray paints for an even coverage. Clean rust off old metal or enamel boxes with a wire brush and wet-and-dry paper, then apply a coat of spray metal primer.

GLASS Glass boxes need minimal preparation and are quick and easy to decorate. Simply paint with glass paints or mask out a design and apply glass etching spray or frosting spray to imitate the effect of etched and sand-blasted glass.

WOVEN The texture of woven boxes can be emphasized by weaving through the surface with raffia or by gluing string designs on top.

box lids

You will need to take into consideration the type of lid the box has. If covering a box with paper or fabric, make sure that a slip-over lid will still fit. The lid of a wooden box can be sanded inside first to make it fit. A new, larger lid can be made for a card box. Just 3mm (1/8in) added to the diameter of a lid can make a significant difference to the ease of the fit. Boxes to be covered with mosaic should have flush-fitting lids.

Gather together an assortment of vibrant and textural materials and accessories to incorporate into or even inspire your designs.

card and decorative papers

Square and rectangular boxes can be made from heavier-weight card than round and oval boxes where the card needs to bend smoothly. Cover and line boxes with specialist handmade papers or colourful giftwrap. Use foil sweet wrappers or fine paper biscuit wrappers to decorate gift boxes.

fabric

Most fabrics are suitable for covering boxes but avoid very thick fabrics, since the box will lose its definition and the lid will be difficult to fit. Fine, loosely woven fabrics are also difficult to work with. Silk dupion is an ideal fabric because it has a crisp texture. A length of ribbon can be glued over the raw edge on the inside of a fabric covering or box lining.

clay and metal

Air-drying clay is available from art and craft shops in natural white or terracotta. The clay can be painted but the terracotta colour is very attractive left unpainted. Polymer clay is available in a huge range of colours that can be mixed. It is hardened by baking in a domestic oven for a short time. Motifs cut from fine sheet metals can be easily embossed with an everyday ballpoint pen. Transfer gold leaf is very luxurious and is used for gilding – a fine craft in its own right.

paints

Acrylic and craft paints are highly versatile. They come in a wide intermixable range of colours, give good coverage and dry quickly. Left-over household emulsion paint can be put to effective use, or choose from the variety of sample pots available at hardware stores. Spray paints come in lots of colours and even pearlized finishes. Protect the surrounding area with scrap paper or newspaper and always spray in a well-ventilated room. Use fabric paints and fabric relief pens to decorate fabric. Easy to use, they can transform a plain fabric into something very special.

natural materials

Incorporate driftwood, twigs, feathers, shells and pebbles in your decorative schemes, to provide interesting textures and a link with the natural world. Do not remove shells and pebbles from beaches. A wonderful variety can be found in specialist shell shops, often situated in holiday resorts. Garden centres stock stones and pebbles in all kinds of sizes and colours.

decorative details

Use oddments of fabric trimmings for additional decoration, including buttons, jewellery stones and different types of ribbon, braid and lace.

techniques

The same basic techniques occur in many of the projects and are described in this section, and the tools required will be in your Basic Tool Kit (see page 9). Always read through the instructions for a project before embarking on it – have some scrap paper to hand for making notes – and try out new techniques on spare scraps of materials first.

When creating a project, it is important to use either metric or imperial measurements but not a combination of both.

using templates

Trace the design onto tracing paper. Turn the tracing over and redraw it on the wrong side with a pencil. Use masking tape to tape the tracing right side up onto the surface. You may want to transfer it to thick paper or thin card to cut out and draw around or transfer it directly onto the material you wish to use. Redraw the design to transfer it.

cutting

Straight edges on paper and card are best cut with a craft knife against a metal ruler resting on a cutting mat. When cutting card, do not press too hard or attempt to cut right through at the first approach, but gradually cut deeper and deeper.

scoring and folding

Scoring card will make it easier to fold and give a neat finish. Thin card can be scored with a craft knife or a bone folder. A bone folder is a traditional bookbinder's tool, and although not essential, it is very useful for scoring. Score with the pointed end of a bone folder against a ruler. Score mounting board with a craft knife against a metal ruler. Take care not to cut right through the card – break the top surface only.

USING TEMPLATES

SCORING AND FOLDING

CUTTING

making a square or rectangular box and lid

Use 300–540gsm weight card for square or rectangular boxes. Refer to the diagrams on page 111 to draw the box to your own dimensions onto card. The front and back must be the same size and the sides the same size.

Draw straight lines against a ruler and use a protractor for accurate right angles. Draw the ends of the tabs at 45-degree angles. Draw the lid and base referring to the box measurements A and B.

1 Cut out the box, base and lid (see Cutting opposite), cutting the lid tabs at a slight angle. Score the lines on the right side and fold backwards along the scored lines (see Scoring and Folding opposite).

2 Apply double-sided tape to the lower tabs on the wrong side and the end tab on the right side of the box. Peel the backing off the tape on the lower tabs and stick them under the base.

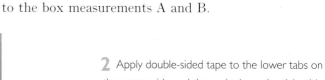

3 Peel the backing tape off the end tab and stick it under the opposite edge of the box.

4 Apply double-sided tape to the tabs of the lid on the right side. Peel off the backing and stick the tabs under the adjacent end of the rim.

making a round or oval box and lid

Use 300gsm weight card, which is similar to the card that cereal packets are made of, to make round and oval boxes, since it is light enough to bend easily but sturdy enough for use as a gift box. To make an oval box, draw an oval instead of a circle for the base and lid.

1 On card, draw a circle with a pair of compasses to the required diameter of your box, for the base. For the box side, cut a strip of card the box height plus 1.5cm (⅝in) by the circumference plus 2.5cm (1in). Score a line parallel with the long edges 1.5cm (⅝in) above the lower long edge for the tabs. Fold backwards along the scored line. Apply double-sided tape along the tabs and to one short edge on the wrong side. Cut off the lower tabs 2.5cm (1in) along from the untaped short end. Snip the tabs to the scored line at 6mm (¼in) intervals, cutting away 'V' shapes.

3 To make the lid, draw around the base of the box onto card adding a 2mm (⅛in) allowance to the circumference and cut out. For the rim, cut a strip of card the depth of the lid plus 1.5cm (⅝in) by the circle circumference plus 2.5cm (1in). Score a line parallel with the long edges 1.5cm (⅝in) above the lower long edge for the tabs. Fold backwards along the scored line.

2 Peel off the backing from the tape. Starting at the untaped short end, wrap the strip around the base, sticking the tabs under the base. Overlap the short edges of the strip and stick together.

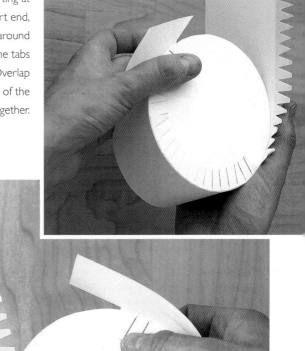

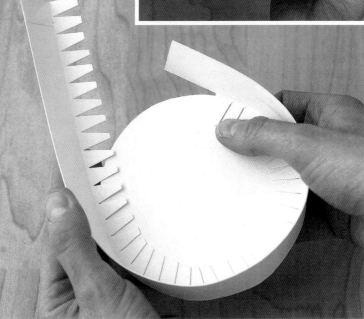

4 Apply double-sided tape along the tabs and to one short edge on the right side. Cut off the lower tabs 2.5cm (1in) along from the untaped short end. Snip the tabs to the scored line at 6mm (¼in) intervals, cutting away 'V' shapes as before. Stick the tabs under the lid starting at the untaped end. Overlap the ends and stick together.

Lining boxes

If you intend to line a box with paper or fabric, do so before covering the exterior. Many of the projects show how to line a box (see Index, page 112).

covering a box with paper

Cover a plain box with an attractive paper, such as giftwrap or wallpaper, to give it an instant makeover.

2 Stick the paper inside the upper edge. Snip the lower edge of the paper at regular intervals on round and oval boxes. Stick the paper under the base, folding under the corners on square and rectangular boxes in neat mitres. To neaten the base, cut a piece of paper 6mm (¼in) smaller on all sides than the base. Stick under the box with spray mount adhesive.

| Cut a strip of paper the circumference of the box plus 2cm (¾in) by the height of the box plus 3cm (1¼in). Spray the wrong side with spray mount adhesive. Wrap the strip around the box with 1.5cm (⅝in) extending above and below the box.

covering a box with fabric

Boxes can be covered with fabric to coordinate with the décor of an interior, or to create a luxurious effect.

2 Glue the fabric inside the upper edge with PVA or white glue. Snip the lower edge of the fabric at regular intervals on round and oval boxes. Stick the fabric under the base, folding under the fullness at the corners in neat mitres on square and rectangular boxes. To neaten the base, cut a piece of fabric 6mm (¼in) smaller on all sides than the base. Stick under the box with art and hobby spray adhesive.

| Cut a strip of fabric the circumference of the box plus 2.5cm (1in) by the height of the box plus 3cm (1¼in). Press 1.5cm (⅝in) to the wrong side at one short edge. Stick in place with PVA or white glue. Wrap the fabric around the box with 1.5cm (⅝in) extending above and below the box. Overlap the short raw edge with the neatened edge and glue in place.

covering a square or rectangular lid with paper or fabric

Different techniques are required if you are covering a lid with either paper or fabric.

1 Cut a square or rectangle of paper the size of the lid with the depth of the rim plus 1.2cm (½in) added to each edge, or cut a square or rectangle of fabric the size of the lid with twice the depth of the rim measurement plus 1cm (⅜in) added to each edge. Spray the wrong side of the paper or fabric with spray mount adhesive. Place the lid face down centrally on the wrong side of the paper or fabric. Snip from the paper or fabric corners to the lid corners.

2 For a paper-covered lid, stick two opposite edges to the rim, sticking the extending ends around the corners. Cut off the remaining diagonal edges. Stick the paper to the remaining sides. Stick the paper inside the lid rim, snipping the paper to the corners to avoid creasing it.

3 For a fabric-covered lid, trim the corner cuts to 1cm (⅜in) beyond the lid corners. Lay the fabric on one side against the rim, sticking the extending ends around the corners with PVA or white glue. Repeat on the opposite side.

4 Turn under 1cm (⅜in) on the trimmed ends of the fabric and stick in place with PVA or white glue. Lift the edges and stick to the remaining uncovered sides of the rim by gluing the turned-under ends along the lid corners. Turn the fabric to the inside of the rim and glue in place, extending the raw edges of the fabric onto the underside of the lid.

covering a round or oval lid with paper or fabric

Even covering only the lid of a plain box is an effective way to add an instant touch of class.

1 Cut a circle or oval of paper or fabric the size of the lid with 1.5cm (⅝in) added to the circumference. Place the lid face down centrally on the wrong side. Snip into the circumference at regular intervals to within 2mm (⅟₁₆in) of the lid. Stick the snipped edges to the rim with PVA or white glue.

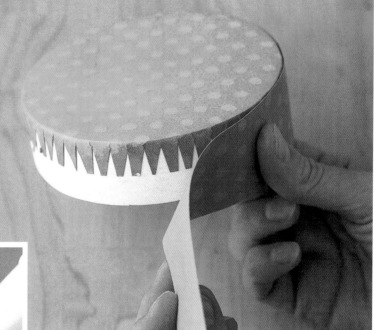

2 For a paper-covered lid, cut a strip of paper the circumference of the lid plus 2cm (¾in) by the rim depth plus 1.2cm (½in). Stick to the rim using spray mount adhesive, matching the upper edges. Stick the lower edge inside the lid.

3 For a fabric-covered lid, cut a strip of fabric the circumference of the lid plus 3cm (1¼in) by twice the rim depth plus 2.5cm (1in). Cut a strip of medium-weight iron-on interfacing the circumference of the lid by the rim depth. Fuse to the wrong side of the fabric 1.5cm (⅝in) inside the upper edge and one end. Press this end and the upper edge of the fabric over the interfacing. Using PVA or white glue, stick the strip around the rim starting at the raw end and with the upper edges level. Overlap the raw end with the pressed end. Stick the lower edge inside the rim and onto the underside of the lid. If the lid is unlined, cut a circle of paper or fabric the same size as the inside of the lid and stick inside with art and hobby spray adhesive.

multi media

multi
media

Almost any material can be used to decorate a box, as long as it is an appropriate weight for the box medium. So look out for the creative potential in all manner of paper-based items, components and accessories, which can also be enhanced by a whole range of craft techniques.

Here, wooden mouldings from a hardware shop are glued to a plain box, then the whole surface gilded, to produce a rich, antiqued finish. Printed biscuit wrappings make an unexpected yet highly effective box covering, while wood-veneer papers are used to create a convincing marquetry effect. Motifs adorning a metal canister have been cut from fine metal and embossed with a ballpoint pen.

Try using a tomato puree tube for crafting decorative motifs, embossing a design on the deep golden metal inside. Other kinds of printed paper – evocative mementos such as luggage labels, postcards, even travel tickets – can be pasted onto a plain box, then varnished for protection. Broken jewellery can be taken apart and the beads used for decoration, for instance in the project on pages 40–3, or glue broken watch and clock parts at random to a container or interesting old keys to the lid of a sturdy box. The possibilities are limitless!

embossed
metal canister

THE CRAFT OF EMBOSSING metal has long been a traditional pastime in Mexico, where it often appears in the 'Day of the Dead' festivities. Today, its popularity is widespread because such effective results can be achieved so quickly. Short lengths of fine metal are available from craft shops or suppliers not only in the usual brass, copper and aluminium finishes but also in vibrant primary colours.

This metal canister is given a new lease of life with a change of colour and a spattering of gold paint. A frieze of curling stylized leaves, worked in embossed metal, is then applied to the surface. A useful airtight container for food storage, the canister makes an eye-catching accessory for the kitchen.

embossed
metal canister

you will need

scrap paper or newspaper

metal canister with lid, at
least 10cm (4in) in diameter

metallic blue spray paint

gold oil-based paint

old toothbrush

sheet of fine brass

old pair of scissors

kitchen paper

step-by-step instructions

1 Protecting the
surrounding area with
scrap paper or newspaper
and working in a well-
ventilated room, spray the
outside of the canister and
lid with metallic blue spray
paint. Leave to dry.

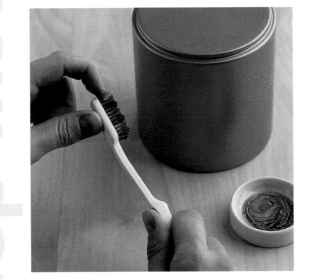

2 Pick up a little oil-
based gold paint on an
old toothbrush. Hold the
brush in one hand, and
with the other hand, pull
back the bristles to spatter
the canister randomly
with paint. Allow to dry.

tip

> Any old, dried-up
ballpoint pen can be
used for embossing.
Although the metal
is thin enough to
cut with a pair of
scissors, use an old
pair since the metal
will blunt the blades.

3 Trace the leaf and
round motif templates
on page 104 onto tracing
paper and cut out. Tape
the tracings onto the metal
with masking tape. Draw
around the templates with
a ballpoint pen, lightly
embossing the surface
of the metal.

4 Remove the tape and cut out the motifs using an old pair of scissors. Repeat to cut out as many leaf motifs as required to fit around the canister; only a single round motif is needed for the lid.

variations

The embossed motifs can be spray-painted before gluing them to the box. Additionally, glue on jewellery stones with all-purpose household glue to add sparkle to the designs. For an alternative look, use the shell motifs on page 104 in place of the leaf and round motifs.

5 Rest the motifs on a few sheets of kitchen paper and draw a decorative design on each motif with a ballpoint pen, pressing down hard to emboss the metal. If you prefer not to draw freehand, replace the tracings and trace along the lines of the designs given.

6 Slip the lid onto the canister. Arrange the leaf motifs around the side of the canister and stick lightly in place with masking tape. Glue to the canister with all-purpose household glue. Glue the round motif to the lid.

gilded celtic
coffret

GILDING IS A CLASSICAL CRAFT that produces exquisite effects. Transfer gold leaf is a layer of gossamer-fine metal on a paper backing. To apply the metal, the surface to be gilded is first coated with 15-minute size, then the metal pressed on top and the backing paper peeled away.

A humble wooden box is embellished with glued-on wooden Celtic-style motifs, and then painted with red oxide paint. Once applied, the gilding is gently distressed so that underlying areas of the deep, rich red are visible.

This charming container would make an elegant addition to a mantelpiece or a desk – ideal for storing candles or keeping household keys safely together in one place.

gilded celtic
coffret

you will need

wooden box with lid

5 wooden Celtic-style bosses
(ornamental mouldings)

wood glue

scrap paper or newspaper

red oxide spray primer

15-minute water-based size

flat paintbrush

transfer gold leaf

small artist's paintbrush

wire wool

methylated spirit

french polish

soft cloth

yellow ochre acrylic paint

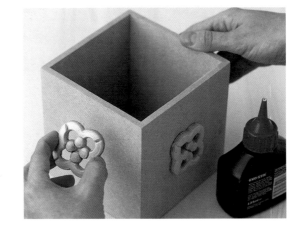

1 Glue a wooden boss to the centre of each side of the box and lid with wood glue. Leave the glue to dry overnight. Protecting the surrounding area with scrap paper or newspaper and working in a well-ventilated room, spray the outside of the box and lid with red oxide primer.

2 Leave the primer to dry, then apply the size to the top of the lid with a flat paintbrush. Set aside for 15–25 minutes, until the size becomes clear and tacky.

3 Lay a sheet of transfer gold leaf over the top of the lid, gold side down. Gently smooth it down onto the size, then peel off the backing paper.

4 Use a small artist's paintbrush to press the metal into the recesses of the boss. Press smaller pieces of left-over metal into the gaps until the item is covered. Brush away the excess metal with the cleaned, dried paintbrush. Do not worry if tiny areas of the red oxide are visible, since the red will show through when the gold leaf is distressed.

5 Gild the box in the same way, working on one side at a time. Moisten wire wool with a little methylated spirit and gently rub the lid and box along the edges where they would receive wear naturally.

6 Add a few drops of French polish to a soft cloth and use to polish the gilding all over the box and lid.

7 Using the flat paintbrush, paint the underside of the lid and the inside of the box with yellow ochre acrylic paint. Leave to dry.

variations

┄┄► *Wooden ornamental mouldings, or bosses, are available in many different styles and forms from hardware stores. Other period examples include a Tudor rose, Georgian scroll and Medieval fleur-de-lys. They also offer a range of contemporary motifs, such as fruit — an appropriate choice for a kitchen container — as well as fish and a seahorse, which would suit a bathroom setting.*

paper marquetry
chess box

THE INSPIRATION for this project comes from the traditional Moorish designs worked in wood marquetry found in Morocco, where intricate geometric shapes are precision-cut by hand from a variety of wood veneers and painstakingly pieced together.

Here, beautiful wood-veneer papers are incorporated into an elegant games box to create a Moorish marquetry effect. The lid has a chessboard design that can be played upon, since many coats of hard-wearing varnish will protect the delicate papers from damage. The box is lined with snakeskin-effect paper.

paper marquetry
chess box

you will need

wood-veneer papers in two finishes, e.g. mahogany and birch

wooden box with lid of light-coloured wood, e.g. pine

plastic glue spreader or strip of card

flat paintbrush

kitchen paper

clear satin polyurethane varnish

varnishing brush

fine glasspaper

snakeskin-effect paper

I Using the templates on page 105, trace the motifs onto tracing paper. Trace the box and lid side designs onto tracing paper folded in half, with the broken lines placed along the fold, to make a complete pattern. Cut out as a strip. Transfer each individual motif onto the wrong side of the wood-veneer papers. Cut out using a craft knife and resting on a cutting mat, cutting straight lines against a metal ruler.

2 Tape the lid tracings to the lid along one edge with masking tape, as a guide to positioning the pieces. Working on one piece at a time, paste the wrong side of the lid veneer pieces with PVA or white glue. Lift the tracing and slip the pieces underneath. Press in position. Wipe off excess glue with moistened kitchen paper. First, stick on all the lid side pieces, cutting the straight strips to size for the short sides, then the lid top pieces.

3 Tape the box side tracing to one side of the box along one edge with masking tape. Paste the wrong side of the relevant veneer pieces with PVA or white glue and stick in place. Repeat on all sides of the box.

4 Remove the tracings and leave the glue to dry for a day. Using a varnishing brush, coat the box and lid with varnish. Leave to dry, then lightly sand the surface with fine glasspaper. Apply a further four coats of varnish, sanding lightly between coats.

tip

Inexpensive wood-veneer and animal-skin-effect papers are available at specialist handmade paper shops and major art and craft stores. The lid of the box shown here is 33.5 x 27cm (13¼ x 10⅝in); simply adjust the size of the templates to suit your own box.

5 Cut a square or rectangle of snakeskin-effect paper 1cm (⅜in) larger on all sides than the inside box base. Spray the wrong side with art and hobby spray adhesive and stick centrally onto the box base. Snip to the corners and press the paper neatly along the edges and onto the inner sides.

6 Cut two strips of snakeskin-effect paper measuring half the circumference of the box plus 2cm (¾in) by the inside height of the box. Spray the wrong side with the spray adhesive. Stick the strips inside the box, matching the upper edges and overlapping the ends. Repeat to line the lid.

italian-wrap hanging boxes

italian-wrap
hanging boxes

THE PRETTILY PRINTED and gossamer-thin wrappers from Italian amaretti – traditional Italian almond-flavoured biscuits – are used to cover dainty hexagonal boxes. They are trimmed with handmade golden tassels and a cord handle, which allows the boxes to be suspended, for instance from a Christmas tree or from silver-painted branches for a celebratory occasion. The petite scale of the boxes is just right to present a special diminutive gift. They could also be used for wedding favours.

Five wrappers will cover two boxes, so you have a good excuse to indulge your taste buds!

italian-wrap
hanging boxes

you will need

thin card

bone folder (optional)

amaretti biscuit wrappers

awl

gold cord

gold stranded cotton
embroidery thread

gold lurex embroidery thread

tapestry needle

variation

➤ *Cover these tiny
gift boxes with
photocopies of a
marriage service
to contain wedding
favours.*

1 Use the templates on page 104 to cut the box side, base, lid side and lid from thin card with a craft knife and resting on a cutting mat. Score along the broken lines with a bone folder or craft knife. Fold along the scored lines. Stick the lower tabs of the box side onto the base and the end tab inside the opposite end with double-sided adhesive tape. Construct the lid in the same way, sticking the upper tabs to the lid underside.

2 Cut one wrapper in half. Spray the wrong side of the wrapper strips with spray mount adhesive. Stick the strips around the sides of the box, overlapping the strip ends. Snip the excess wrapper to the base corners, then stick smoothly onto the base underside. Trim the remaining excess wrapper level with the upper edge of the box.

3 Spray the wrong side of one wrapper with spray mount adhesive. Stick the wrapper centrally onto the lid, smoothing outwards from the centre. Snip to the corners. Stick the excess wrapper to the sides, overlapping the cut edges at the corners. Trim the excess wrapper level with the lower edge of the lid. Cut a base from a wrapper, trimming 6mm (¼in) from the edges. Stick to the base underside with spray mount adhesive.

4 Using an awl, pierce a hole at the dots on the box. To form a handle, thread a 30cm (12in) length of gold cord through the holes, knotting the ends inside the box. To make a tassel, cut a rectangle of thin card 10 x 5cm (4 x 2in) and fold in half, short edges together. Wind gold stranded cotton and lurex embroidery thread together over the folded edge.

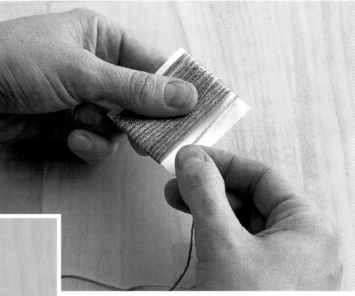

5 Fold a strand of gold embroidery thread about 45cm (18in) in length in half, then thread the ends through the eye of a tapestry needle. Thread the needle behind the strands close to the fold. Insert the needle through the loop of the yarn and pull tightly to suspend the tassel.

6 Slip a blade of the sharp scissors between the two layers of card, and cut through all the loops of embroidery thread. Discard the card.

7 Thread a single length of yarn onto the needle, then bind tightly around the head of the tassel. Insert the needle into the bulk of the tassel to secure and to lose the end of the thread within the tassel. Cut the lower edge of the tassel level. Tie a tassel to each end of the handle. Poke the tying threads through the box holes, then trim the ends.

oriental etched pot

oriental
etched pot

THE DELICATE EFFECT of etched glass is simple to imitate nowadays using a glass etch spray, widely available from art and craft stores or suppliers.

Stylized fronds of bamboo are worked on the front of this coolly sophisticated glass box, with a single stem on the other sides. The motifs are masked out using sticky-backed plastic, and the box is then sprayed with the etch spray. Finally the mask is pulled away to reveal the design left beneath.

Perfect for the bathroom, the box can be filled with cotton wool. Alternatively, swirl in a plain-coloured silk scarf as an extra gift and to highlight the design.

oriental
etched pot

you will need

sticky-backed plastic

glass box with lid,
approximately 12cm (4¾in)
high and 11cm (4¼in) wide

item taller than box to
support it while applying
the glass etch spray

glass etch spray

scrap paper or newspaper

tip

➤ *When using glass
etch spray, apply in
thin coats of spray
rather than one
heavy coat. Set the
box aside after a
few coats, since the
etched effect will
intensify as it dries,
then carefully peel
back a corner of the
stencil to check the
result and whether
to apply more coats.*

1 Using the template on
page 106, trace the motif
onto tracing paper. Transfer
one whole design to the
paper backing of the sticky-
backed plastic and three of
just the right-hand, more
upright stem. Resting on
a cutting mat, cut out the
individual pieces of the
motifs with a craft knife.

2 Make sure the glass
is clean and free from
grease. Tape the tracing for
the front inside the front
of the box with masking
tape. Peel the backing
paper off the front motif
pieces and stick in place
on the outside of the box.
Remove the tracing.

3 Tape the tracing inside one side of the box. Stick the single stem sticky-backed pieces in place as before. Remove the tracing and repeat on the other sides.

4 Upturn the box and slip it over a taller item so that the rim of the box does not rest on the work surface. Cover the surrounding area with scrap paper or newspaper. Spray the box with glass etch spray following the manufacturer's instructions.

5 Leave the box to dry thoroughly, then carefully peel off all the plastic pieces.

variation

⋯⋯▶ *Swirling butterflies would make an effective alternative etched-glass design. Use the template on page 106 to apply a pair of butterflies to the front of the box, and single ones to the other sides.*

contemporary beaded basket

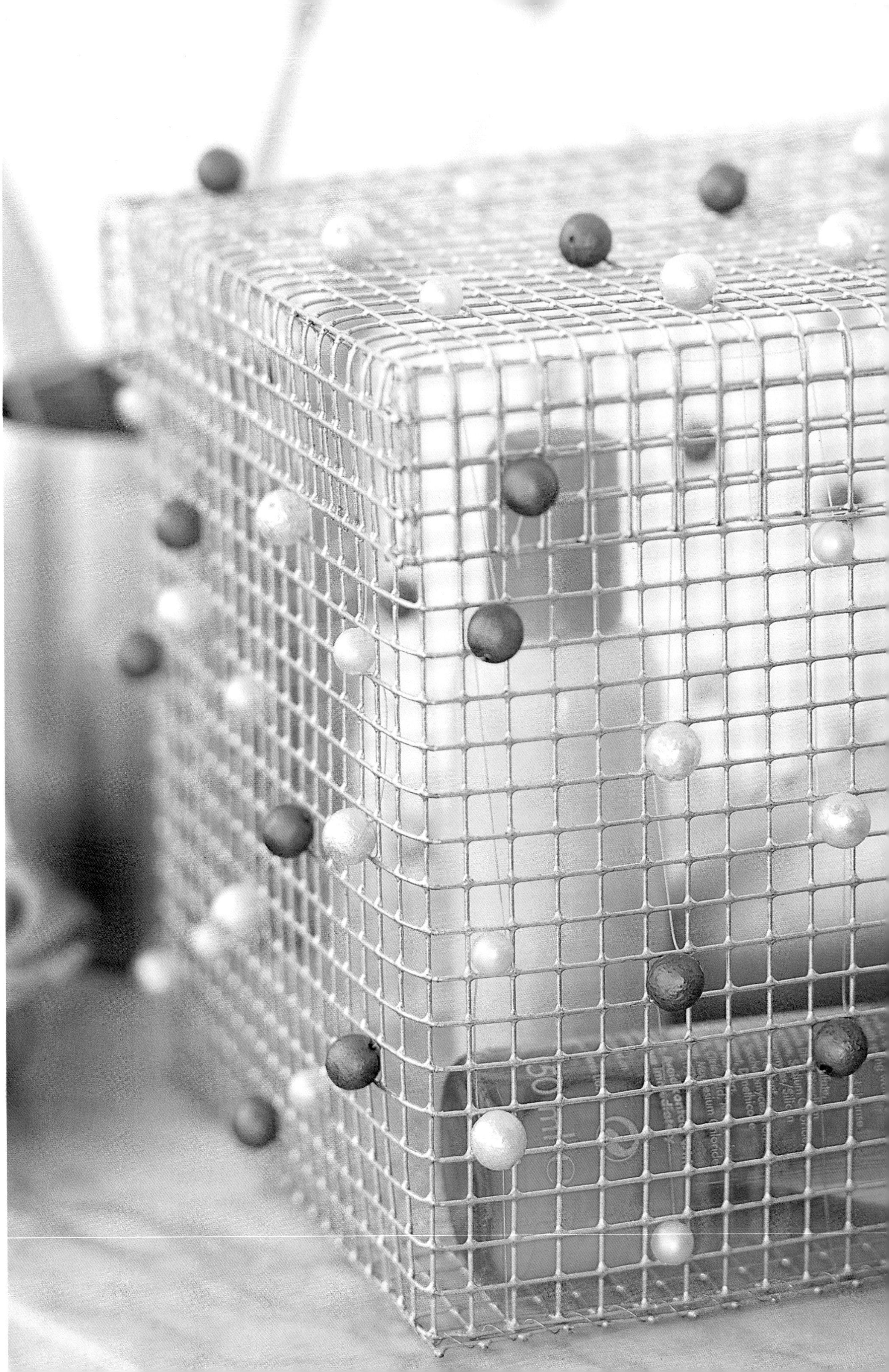

contemporary
beaded basket

CREATE A CUTTING-EDGE, 'designer'

accessory to adorn a style-conscious

bathroom. Use it to store and display

colourful, shaped or fragrant soaps, or

other small-scale toiletries.

The container is made from wire

mesh available from hardware stores and

garden centres. Any size square mesh can

be used, since it's the number of squares

that is relevant, not their size. Easy to

handle, the mesh can be snipped to size

and folded into shape. Fine wire is then

used to join the pieces together. Dainty

pearl beads are interlaced through the

mesh as a contrast to the defined lines

of the mesh.

contemporary
beaded basket

you will need

tin snips, wire cutters or an old, large pair of scissors

sheet of 22 gauge or fine square wire mesh

fine wire, e.g. fuse wire

pearl beads in three colours, 6mm (¼in) and 8mm (5⁄16in) in diameter

5½m (6yd) fishing line or nylon thread

tip

> *If the mesh edges are rough after cutting, file them smooth with a metal file.*

| Use tin snips, wire cutters or an old, large pair of scissors to snip a strip of wire mesh 80 squares long by 20 squares deep, snipping the mesh just beyond the edges of the squares. To form the box shape, fold the mesh against a ruler to make four 20 × 20 squares for each side.

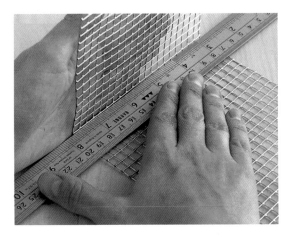

2 Starting at the upper edge, lace the meeting edges together with fine wire. Bind the wire through the top squares a few times to secure them together. Leave the wire extending at the lower edge ready for joining the base.

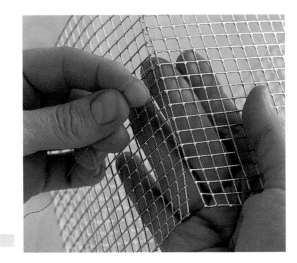

3 Snip a square of mesh for the base 20 squares deep by 20 squares wide. Place against the lower edge of the box and use the extending wire to lace the edges together. Bind the wire a few times through the last squares to secure the join, then snip off the excess wire.

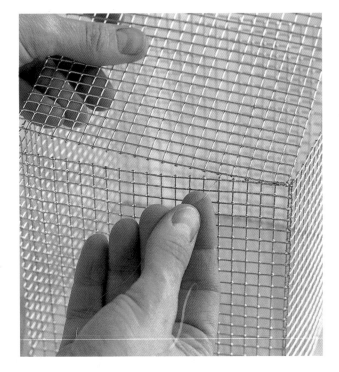

4 Snip a square of mesh for the lid 29 squares deep by 29 squares wide. Snip away 4 × 4 squares at each corner. Fold up each side of the lid to form a rim 4 squares deep, again folding against a ruler to achieve even edges.

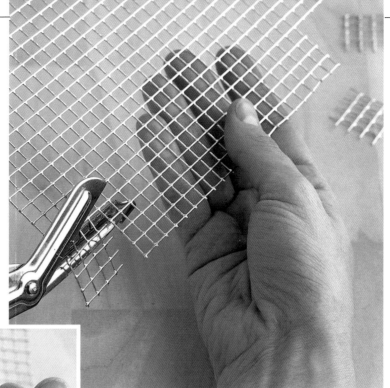

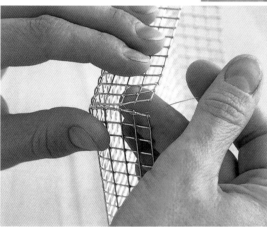

5 Lace the meeting edges of the rim together with fine wire, binding the wire through the top and bottom squares to secure the join. Snip off the excess wire.

variations

Use small decorative buttons in place of the pearl beads. Alternatively, drill holes through a collection of tiny shells for threading onto the fishing line or nylon thread.

6 Fasten a long length of fishing line or nylon thread to the upper edge of the box. Weave the line in and out of the squares, down and up the box sides, threading on beads at random and placing them at least 4 squares below the upper edge to allow for the lid. Tie the end of the line or thread to the box and trim the excess. Decorate the lid in the same way.

fanciful
cake cups

THESE ARE THE ULTIMATE in novelty
cakes – and they're kind to the waistline
too! Each box resembles a corrugated
metal cup cake container. This is achieved
by painting a band of corrugated card
with metallic spray paints. The box lids
are layered with highly realistic chocolate
and cream, then topped with tempting
cherries modelled from coloured
polymer clay, which is baked to harden
in a domestic oven.

Fill these fun containers with
colourful confectionery – perhaps even
homemade sweets or chocolates – to
delight younger members of your family
or your friends.

fanciful
cake cups

you will need

thin card

single-wall corrugated card

paper clip

scrap paper or newspaper

metallic spray paint

gummed paper tape

white, brown and red polymer clay

rolling pin

bread board

small kitchen knife

medium-sized round artist's paintbrush

baking sheet

water-based matt varnish

water-based gloss varnish

1 To construct the box, cut a circle of card for the base 6cm (2⅜in) in diameter and a strip for the side of the box 20.5 × 5.5cm (8¼ × 2¼in). Follow Steps 1–2 on page 14 to make a round box. Cut a strip of single-wall corrugated card 22 × 3cm (8 × 1¼in). Stick the corrugated card around the box with the lower edges level and overlapping the ends using all-purpose household glue. Secure the join with a paper clip while the glue dries. Turn the box upside down and rest it on scrap paper or newspaper and spray-paint a metallic colour.

2 Cut a circle of card for the lid 6.3cm (2½in) in diameter and a strip for the lid rim 22 × 1.5cm (8⅝ × ⅝in). Pull the strip between your fingers to curve it. Cut 6mm (¼in) wide pieces of gummed paper tape. Wrap the card strip around the lid and stick in place with the pieces of tape. Stick a 1.5cm (⅝in) piece of tape over the overlapped ends.

tip

The realistic corrugated containers are made from single-wall corrugated card. This is card that is corrugated on one side only, allowing the card to bend.

3 For each cake, roll a 1.2cm (½in) diameter log of brown clay for the 'chocolate' on a cutting mat or bread board. Flatten with a rolling pin to 6mm (¼in) thick. Wrap the clay around the lid, cut the ends level with a small kitchen knife and butt them together. Smooth over the join with a finger to merge the cut ends seamlessly.

4 Roll a 3.5cm (1⅜in) diameter ball of white and brown clay. Flatten with your fist, then roll each piece out flat to 6mm (¼in) thick with a rolling pin to form a disc. Place the white disc on the lid and gently press the edges onto the 'chocolate'. Place the brown disc on top and gently press it down in the centre to fuse it to the white clay.

variations

Instead of placing a cherry on top of the cakes, sprinkle on tiny pieces cut from pastel-coloured clay to look like 'hundreds and thousands', or grate some brown clay on top to represent slivers of chocolate. Lightly press the pieces in position before baking.

5 Roll a 2cm (¾in) diameter ball of red clay for a cherry. Make a dent across the top with the handle end of a round artist's paintbrush. Press onto the top of the cake. Transfer the lids to a baking sheet and bake in a domestic oven following the clay manufacturer's instructions. Allow to cool. Varnish the cake with matt varnish and the cherry with gloss varnish using the artist's paintbrush.

organic options

organic options

The natural world provides endless inspiration and a wonderful source of materials for decorating boxes, but remember to collect only fallen leaves and flowers from the wild. Pebbles, shells and feathers are available from craft shops and specialist suppliers, to bring texture and interest to plain containers. To create lighter, more delicate designs for gift boxes, use PVA (white) glue to apply pressed flowers, leaves and leaf skeletons. Add a coat of varnish or a layer of transparent paper or fabric to protect them.

But why not start with the down-to-earth approach. Here, a casket is made entirely from slabs of clay 'weathered' by a lichen-effect paint treatment. Alternatively, clay can be shaped or sculptured, as in the Beehive project on pages 70–3. A ready-made box of woven rattan is appropriately enhanced with a coarse string design. Continue the natural theme by attaching handles and knobs made from wood or clay.

Unglazed ceramic pieces offer much scope for creating stylized mosaic designs, such as the classical Greek example on pages 58–61. Chips of blue and white china sometimes found when digging in the garden and tide-smoothed glass fragments can also be used. To avoid warping a lightweight box, apply painted balsa wood shapes cut with a craft knife.

beachcomber
box

THIS SEASHORE-INSPIRED box is painted in subtle hues of lilac and pale green. Tile adhesive is applied in a wave design on the sides of the box, and a collection of pretty pebbles are pressed into it. The handle is an attractive piece of driftwood fastened to the lid with leather thonging.

The box can used for creatively preserving treasured holiday memories or keepsakes from travels afar, so that the experience can be recaptured and relived time and time again. To complete the gift, place a scrapbook album inside for mounting snapshots, postcards, maps and leaflets from historical sites, or a holiday diary for recording a vacation to come.

beachcomber
box

you will need

wooden box with lid

lilac and pale green emulsion paint

2.5cm (1in) paintbrush

white all-purpose tile adhesive and grout

tile-adhesive spreader

damp cloth

small pebbles

piece of driftwood

awl or bradawl

drill

leather thonging

1 Paint one side of the box with the emulsion paint, dabbing on the two colours, then blending the shades together on the surface of the wood. Do not overwork the blending but keep the separate colours visible in places. Leave to dry, then turn the box to continue painting. Paint the lid in the same way to match.

2 Spread the tile adhesive about 6mm (¼in) thick in an irregular wave design along the lower third of the box on one side using a tile-adhesive spreader. Wipe off any spills immediately with a damp cloth. Draw the spreader over the adhesive to even the surface.

variations

...➤ *Shells also work well with this technique. If you wish, use a coloured grout to create a contrast to the pieces you are embedding. Alternatively, spray-paint the pebbles before embedding them. Rich, metallic shades would be especially effective.*

3 Gather together pebbles of a similar size and thickness. Press an arrangement of pebbles into the adhesive. Leave to dry thoroughly, then repeat on the other sides of the box. Work quickly before the adhesive starts to set.

4 Arrange the driftwood centrally on the lid. Using an awl or bradawl, pierce a pair of holes in the box lid either side of the driftwood and towards each end of the driftwood. Remove the driftwood. Drill through the pierced holes through the thickness of the lid.

tip

Do not collect your pebbles from the beach but choose from the wide variety now available at garden centres and florists. If using shells instead (see Variations), again avoid collecting from the beach. There are specialist suppliers that offer beautiful selections of shells by mail order, many from exotic corners of the globe.

5 Replace the driftwood on the box lid. Thread a length of leather thonging through the holes to secure the driftwood. Tie the ends of the thonging together firmly on the underside of the lid. Trim the excess thonging.

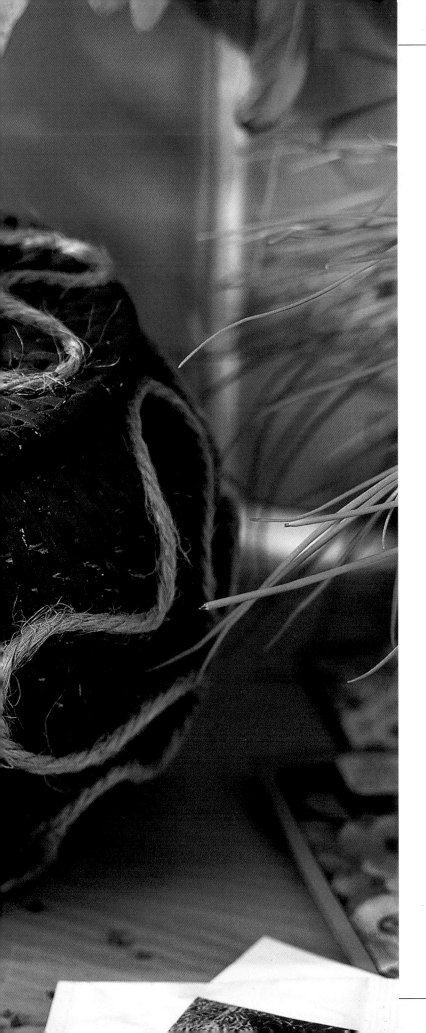

rustic rattan
basket

IN THIS QUICK-TO-CREATE project,

a chunky woven rattan box is given a

simple paint treatment and a fittingly

rustic decoration of string arranged in

a flowing organic design. A plain wooden

household knob is bound with string and

attached to the lid. A tatty or damaged

box can be disguised by coiling string

around the entire container and lid, as

on the knob here.

The box offers an appropriate, handy

and attractive storage container for an

indoor gardening kit of raffia and/or string

and gardening scissors. It is also ideal for

storing bulbs, since the rattan lets in air

while they remain excluded from the light

rustic rattan
basket

you will need

stencil brush

brown acrylic paint

rattan box with lid

awl

wooden cupboard knob

ball of string

washer

small screw

screwdriver

cocktail stick or toothpick

step-by-step instructions

I Dip a stencil brush into brown acrylic paint. Dab the paint onto the box and lid, both inside and out. Move the brush around to work the paint into the weave of the box. Set aside to dry.

2 Use an awl to make a hole in the top of the knob. Dab all-purpose household glue onto the end of the string. Allow to dry, then cut to a point to stiffen the end. Insert the stiffened end into the hole.

variations

⤏ *This simple idea can be adapted to make lots of different looks. For a contrasting, luxurious effect, try using gold cord on a regal velvet-covered box.*

3 Spread glue onto the knob around the hole. Bind the string around the hole, pressing it onto the knob. Add more glue and completely cover the knob with string. Trim the last line of string level with the lower edge of the knob.

4 Thread a washer onto a small screw. Make a hole in the centre of the lid with the awl. Insert the screw up through the hole from the underside of the lid. Screw on the knob with a screwdriver.

tip

A cocktail stick or toothpick is ideal for applying glue to the string used to create the pattern, since only a small amount is needed to stick the string in place and avoids any visible excess glue on the box surface.

5 Use a cocktail stick or toothpick to run a line of glue in a random pattern on the box, working on a small area at a time so that the glue does not dry out. Press the string onto the glue. Continue until the entire box is covered with the design, then neatly trim the end of the string and secure with glue.

6 Decorate the box lid with string in the same way as the box, again neatly trimming the end of the string and securing with glue. Leave the box and lid to dry.

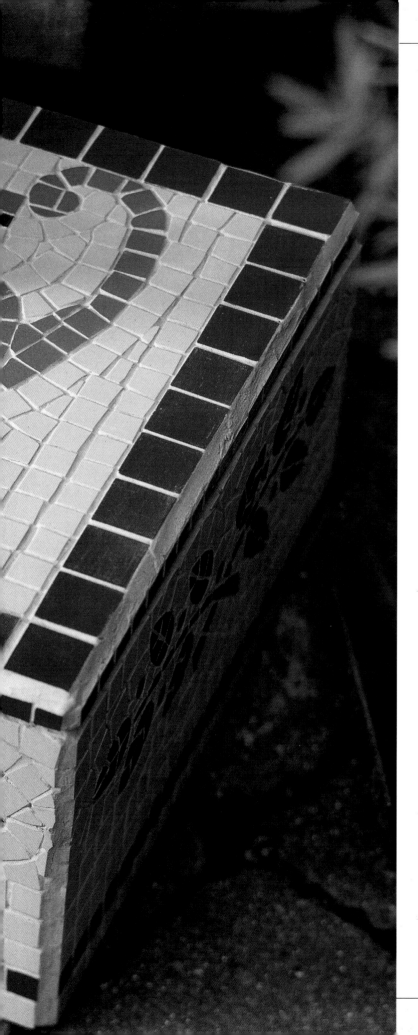

classical
mosaic chest

UNGLAZED CERAMIC SQUARES, known as tesserae, are used to cover a plain wooden box, transforming it into an enduring work of art. The earthy colours and matt finish of the unglazed ceramic pieces add to the authentic effect of an Ancient Greek design.

Most tesserae are sold in sheet form with a paper backing that can be soaked off in water, and are available at specialist mosaic and tile shops.

Sturdy in quality, the box is ideally suited to storing relatively heavy items, such as a gardening set of hand-fork and trowel or bottles of differently flavoured olive oil, in superior style.

classical
mosaic chest

you will need

2.5cm (1in) square unglazed ceramic tesserae in dark red, black, grey and yellow ochre

container of water

wooden box with flush fitting lid, at least 28 x 28cm (11 x 11in)

tile nippers

goggles (optional)

grey powdered grout

grouting squeegee

damp cloth

clean, soft cloth

flat paintbrush

yellow ochre emulsion paint

1 Soak the sheets of tesserae in a container of water for about 10 minutes for the backing paper to peel away. Using the templates on page 107, transfer the urn design to the centre of the lid and the olive branches to each side of the box. Run a line of PVA or white glue along the centre of one border on the lid. Stick a row of dark red tesserae squares on top with a gap of about 3mm (⅛in) between the squares. Continue along all edges of the lid.

2 Practise snipping the squares in half. Hold one tessera square between the thumb and fingers of your left hand, with the thumb running along one edge of the tessera. Slip the nippers about 3mm (⅛in) into the centre from the opposite edge and squeeze them closed to crack the tessera in half. Do not worry if they are not perfect halves. Cut the sections into halves again to make four squares from each tessera square. These are useful sizes to work with and can be nibbled into shape with the nippers.

3 Use the tile nippers to cut a selection of tesserae into quarters. Fill in the urn design, nibbling the pieces to shape where necessary to fit. Either 'butter' each piece with glue or run a line of glue onto the area where the mosaic is to be applied and press the mosaics in position. Most PVA or white glue containers have a narrow nozzle for easy application. Apply the glue generously but not so that it seeps onto the top of the tesserae when stuck down. Fill in the background with yellow ochre pieces.

4 Turn the box onto one side and apply a row of yellow ochre quarter squares along the lower edges, then a row of dark red quarter squares above. Stick the olive branch pieces in place, then fill in the background with yellow ochre pieces. Allow the glue to dry for a few hours before turning the box to repeat on the other sides. Apply a row of dark red quarter squares to the lid rim.

variation

........➤ *The cost of tesserae often varies according to their colour. Shades of blue are plentiful and usually the cheapest to buy due to their customary use in swimming pools. Try working a simple Mackintosh-style design in pale and dark blue using the template on page 107.*

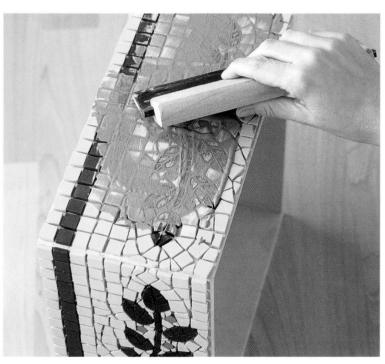

5 Leave the mosaic for 24 hours while the glue dries. Mix the powdered grout with water following the manufacturer's instructions. Starting at one end, spread the grout onto one box side with a squeegee, spreading the grout in all directions so that it fills the gaps between the tesserae pieces. Run your finger along the outer edges to smooth away the excess grout.

safety note

........➤ *When using tile nippers to cut the tesserae to shape, it is advisable to wear goggles for protection.*

6 Wipe away the excess grout with a damp cloth. Work in a small circular motion and rinse the cloth regularly. Continue grouting the other sides, one at a time, then grout the lid. Leave the grout to set for 24 hours, then buff with a clean, soft cloth. Using a flat paintbrush, paint the inside of the box and underside of the lid with yellow ochre emulsion paint.

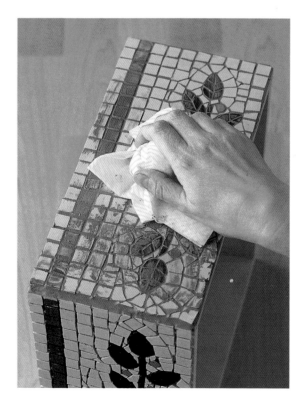

keepsake compartments

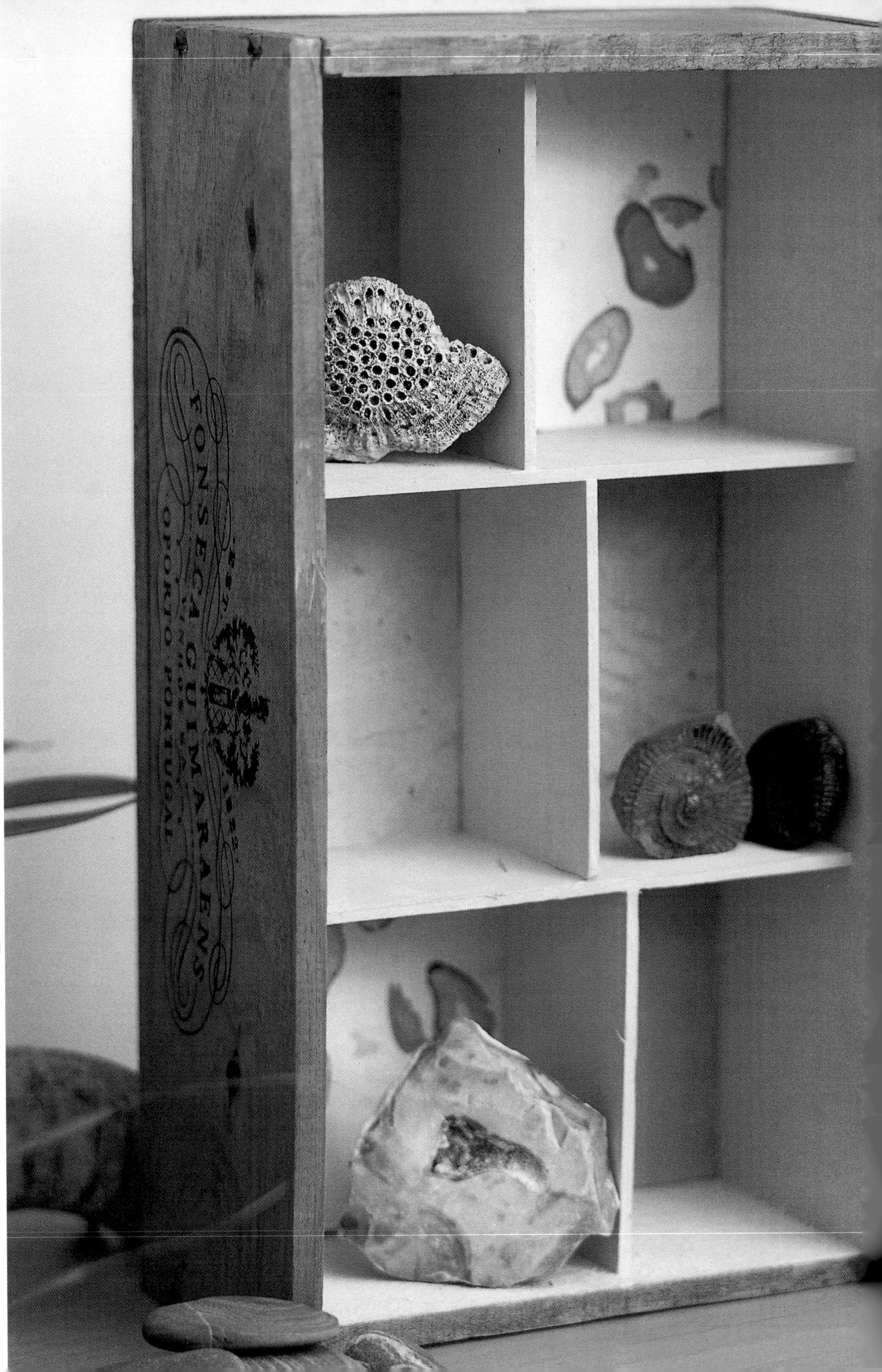

keepsake
compartments

WOODEN PRESENTATION boxes, such as port or wine boxes, are the sort of item that we often hold on to since they are so attractive with their embossed labelling. Boxes with slide-in lids are ideal for turning into distinctive display boxes by simply replacing the wooden lid with a piece of glass.

The exterior of this box is subtly coloured with beeswax blended with artist's oil paint. Inside, compartments are formed from balsa wood to house and display collected treasures, such as interesting beads, or a variety of crystals, gemstones or interesting fossils. Line the compartments with attractive papers textured with natural materials such as slivers of bark and seeds.

keepsake
compartments

you will need

old dish or tub, to mix beeswax and paint

beeswax

cadmium red deep hue oil paint

stick

wine box with slide-in lid or similar

soft cloth

cotton bud

4mm (³⁄₁₆in) thick balsa wood

wood glue

damp cloth

off-white emulsion paint

flat paintbrush

natural-coloured handmade and textured papers

picture glass

1 In an old dish or tub, mix approximately two parts beeswax to one part oil paint using a stick, to colour the beeswax with the paint.

2 Set aside the box lid. Use a soft cloth to rub the mixture onto the outside of the box and the rim. Use a cotton bud to apply the wax to the lid recess. Leave to dry.

3 With a craft knife and resting on a cutting mat, cut two rectangles of balsa wood for the shelves the width of the interior of the box by 1cm (³⁄₈in) less than the depth of the box (from below the recess). Apply wood glue to the lower long edge and both short edges of the shelves. Slide the shelves into the box, dividing it into thirds. Press in place and wipe away any excess glue with a damp cloth.

4 Measure the distance between the shelves. Cut three pieces of balsa wood for the divisions measuring the distance between the shelves by the depth of the shelves. Apply wood glue to the lower edge and both short ends of the divisions. Slide the divisions into the box between the shelves, dividing the box into sections. Press in place and wipe away any excess glue with a damp cloth.

5 Leave the glue to dry overnight. Paint the interior of the box off-white. Although the base of the box will be covered with papers, paint it first so that any pale or thin papers will have an even colouring. Leave to dry.

6 Measure the size of the base of each compartment and cut a piece of paper to fit. Check the fit and adjust if necessary. Stick the papers inside the box with spray mount adhesive. Use the wooden box lid as a template to have a piece of glass cut. Arrange your keepsakes in the compartments, then slide in the glass.

terracotta and lichen casket

THIS RUSTIC CLAY CONTAINER is

modelled from terracotta-coloured clay,

which dries hard naturally in the air. The

interesting motifs on the lid are simply

embossed by pressing a pretty button

into the wet clay, while the distressed

lichen effect is created by randomly

sponging on paint. Strands of raffia tie

the box corners together.

Stylish in design, the casket can

take its useful place in many different

quarters of the home, for instance in the

kitchen for storing bulbs of garlic, or in a

conservatory or workroom for containing

packets of seeds or craft materials such

as origami papers, paints and inks.

terracotta and lichen casket

step-by-step instructions

you will need

terracotta air-drying clay

rolling pin

small kitchen knife

pen top, approximately 1cm (⅜in) in diameter

embossed button

fine glasspaper

2 weighty items, e.g. jam jars

cream and aquamarine acrylic paint

flat paintbrush

ceramic tile or an old plate

natural sponge

raffia

I Roll the clay out flat approximately 8mm (⁵⁄₁₆in) thick on a cutting mat or bread board. Use the template on page 106 to cut four side panels with a kitchen knife, cutting the edges against a ruler. Roll the clay again to cut one 9cm (3½in) square for the base and one 15cm (6in) square for the lid. Roll the clay to 6mm (¼in) thick to cut one 10.5cm (4in) square for the lid support.

tip

A cutting mat is a great surface on which to model this project, since it can be quickly wiped clean and the printed grid on the mat is a useful guide for cutting the angles accurately.

2 Pat the cut edges of the sides and lid with a moistened finger to curve them. Refer to the template to punch a hole at each side of the side panels with a pen top. Twist the top to lift the clay cleanly out of the holes.

3 Press the button firmly onto the centre of the lid to stamp the button motif. Repeat above and below the centre to make a row of three motifs.

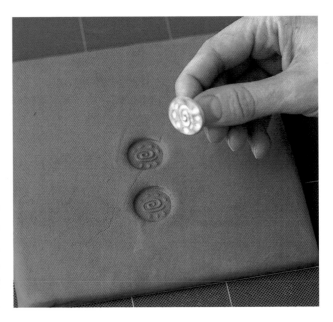

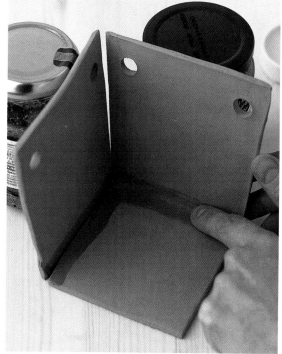

4 Carefully turn the lid over and moisten the underside. Moisten the top of the lid support and press it centrally onto the lid with the moistened sides together. Set all the clay pieces aside to harden, then sand the cut edges with glasspaper to smooth them.

5 Butt two panels upright against the base with the sides adjoining one another. Support the panels against heavy items to hold them in place. Moisten the joins inside the box at the base and smear with clay. Leave to harden, then join the other panels in the same way. Moisten the side edges of the panels and smear with clay to join them. Leave to dry, then moisten and add more clay to strengthen the joins if necessary.

6 Apply cream paint to a ceramic tile or an old plate to use as a palette. Moisten the natural sponge and dab at the paint. Sponge onto the lower half of the box. Apply aquamarine paint in the same way, sponging sparingly on top.

7 Leave the casket to dry thoroughly. Thread strands of raffia through the holes at each corner and tie the ends together on the outside. Trim the excess raffia.

layered beehive pots

layered beehive
pots

THESE APPEALING BEEHIVES are

modelled from coils of air-drying clay built

up in layers. The highly realistic bees that

buzz around the hives, available from

specialist candle shops or suppliers, are

fixed to short wires that are intended to

be inserted into candles. Alternatively, you

could model your own insects from the

air-drying clay and paint accordingly.

Lift off the tops of the hives and the

bases become unique candleholders –

perfect for a duo of sweetly scented

candles. Simply replace the lids when

not in use. Alternatively, fill the hives with

aromatic potpourri and leave the lids ajar

to release the scent.

layered beehive
pots

you will need

air-drying clay

rolling pin

bread board

straight-sided lid about 7cm (2¾in) in diameter and 5.5cm (2¼in) tall

small kitchen knife

petroleum jelly

container of water

baking foil

fine glasspaper

yellow ochre acrylic paint

medium-sized round paintbrush

artificial bees on wires

1 To make a base, roll the clay out flat 6mm (¼in) thick on a cutting mat or bread board. Use the straight-sided lid as a template to cut a round using a kitchen knife. Pull away the excess clay.

2 Smear the sides of the lid with petroleum jelly to act as a releasing agent – the lid will be used as a mould to form the lower section of the beehive. Replace the mould on the clay round (base). Roll 8mm (5⁄16in) diameter logs of clay. Moisten the circumference of the base. Wrap one log around the base. Cut the ends to meet. Moisten the ends and butt them together at the back, forming a ring.

3 Add a second and third ring on top, moistening the top of each preceding ring before applying the next one. Gently press down on the rings to fuse them together. Use the knife to carefully cut out a small opening in the first ring at the front. Remove the mould and set the base aside to harden.

4 To make the lid, roll more logs of clay and wrap them around the mould as before, moistening the top of each previous ring and butting the ends together at the back. Continue to the top of the mould. Scrunch up a piece of baking foil tightly into a dome shape, with the base matching the diameter of the mould. Place on top of the mould and check the shape, squeezing it smaller or enlarging it with more foil if necessary.

tip

The hive is formed over the lid of a can. The lid of a large spray mount adhesive can was used here, but any straight-sided lid or pot would do. Baking foil is then scrunched into a dome to form a mould for the domed top of the hive.

5 Build up the hive shape over the foil mould with decreasing rings of clay, joining the ends at the back as before. Gently press down on the rings to fuse them together. Roll a small ball of clay for the top. Flatten it slightly, moisten and press to the top of the lid. Set aside to harden. If any of the rings are loose, moisten the inside and smear with more clay.

safety note

Never leave a lit candle unattended or replace the lid while the candle is still alight.

6 Sand the top of the box and the lower edge of the lid so that they meet neatly when the lid is placed on the box. Paint the box and lid inside and out. Leave to dry, then push the wire of the bees into the lid between the rings.

textural

textural textiles

textiles

These projects will put to creative use any fabric scraps and related trimmings and accessories. Simply beginning by covering an old or plain box with fabric quickly transforms it and provides the perfect basis for further embellishment. But even before this stage you can introduce decorative effects, for example by first pleating the fabric, as in the project on pages 100–3, or quilting it. Here also, a plain fabric is stamped with an exotic motif and then highlighted with relief pens, which apply a raised line of glitter or pearlized paint. Alternatively, designs could be stencilled onto the fabric or worked in embroidery. A simply embroidered monogram would add a memorable personal note to a gift or wedding box. Add jewellery stones and sequins for extra sparkle and glamour.

Another decorative dimension explored here is applying cutout fabric motifs to a fabric-covered box using bonding web, fused by heat from a domestic iron, which makes the edges resistant to fraying. See also how simply gluing on offcuts of ribbon, braid and lace can almost instantly elevate a ready-made gift box. Remember not to overlook the interior of the box. A padded fabric lining would add a sumptuous finishing touch and give protection to delicate objects and precious jewellery.

beaded dragonfly
jewellery box

THE EXOTIC DRAGONFLY that appears

to have alighted upon this beautiful silk-

covered box is modelled from beads and

jewellery wire. The gossamer-fine wings

are fashioned from iridescent organza

held in shape with wire.

Craft and specialist jewellery shops

stock jewellery wire, and since only

small quantities of materials are needed,

this is a great project to make using any

oddments of fabric, beads and sequins

that you may have to hand.

A suitably elegant box for storing

favourite pieces of jewellery, it could also

be filled with a luxurious scarf for an

extra-special gift.

beaded dragonfly
jewellery box

you will need

round card box, about 15cm (6in) in diameter, with slip-over lid

wallpaper

115g (4oz) wadding

beige silk fabric

medium-weight iron-on interfacing

1cm (⅜in) wide green ribbon

5 gold rocaille beads

0.05mm (1/32in) diameter gold jewellery wire

old scissors or wire cutters

jewellery pliers

super glue

4 × 8mm (5/16in) green beads

2 × 6mm (¼in) green beads

8 × 3mm (⅛in) green beads

scrap paper

8cm (3¼in) square of green organza

awl

6mm (¼in) green sequins

1 To line the box, cut a circle of wallpaper with a diameter 1cm (⅜in) larger than the box base. Spray the wrong side with art and hobby spray adhesive and stick centrally onto the base inside the box. Snip the curves and press the paper neatly around the edge and onto the inner sides. Cut a strip of wallpaper the circumference of the box plus 1.5cm (⅝in) by the inside height of the box less 6mm (¼in). Spray the wrong side with the spray adhesive. Stick the strip inside the box, overlapping the ends.

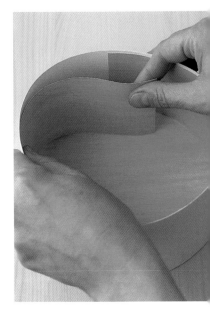

2 Draw around the lid onto wadding with a pen. Cut out and stick to the top of the lid with the spray adhesive. Cover the box and lid with the silk fabric following the techniques on pages 15 and 17. Do not stick the lid liner in position yet. Glue a length of ribbon to cover the raw edge inside the box.

3 To make the dragonfly, thread a gold rocaille bead onto an 18cm (7in) length of jewellery wire. Use a pair of jewellery pliers to bend over the end of the wire to hold it in place. To make the antennae, bend an 8cm (3¼in) length of wire in half, pulling the ends past one another to make a small loop at the centre. Slip the central wire through the loop and push the antennae along the wire to rest against the bead. Squeeze the loop with the pliers to secure it, then dab with super glue. Leave to dry, then bend the antennae forwards and coil the ends with the pliers.

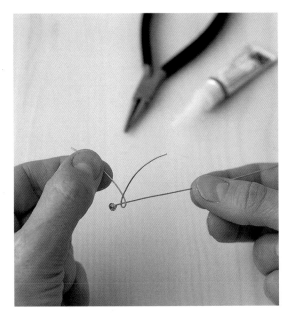

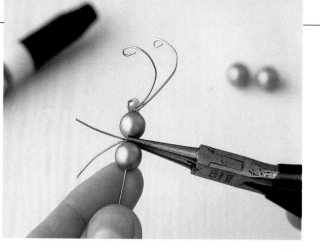

4 Thread on two 8mm (⁵⁄₁₆in) green beads. To make the front legs, bend a 5cm (2in) length of wire in half, making a loop at the centre as before. Slip the loop between the large beads. Squeeze the loop with the pliers to secure it, then dab with super glue. Squeeze the beads together and leave to dry.

5 Bend a length of wire along the outline of the wings template on page 108, crossing the ends at the dot. Place the wire wings on scrap paper and tape over the extending ends below the intersection with masking tape. These will be the legs, with the tape protecting them from glue. Dab with super glue at the intersection but take care not to glue the wire to the paper. Leave to dry. Spray the wings with art and hobby spray adhesive. Remove the tape and press the organza on top. Carefully trim away the organza 2mm (¹⁄₁₆in) beyond the wire.

6 Pull the ends of the legs past each other to make a small loop. To make a third pair of legs, bend a 16cm (6½in) length of wire in half, pulling the ends past one another to make a small loop at the centre. Slip the central wire through the loops of the wings, then the third set of legs. Squeeze the loops with the pliers to secure them, then dab both sets of legs with super glue. Leave to dry, then bend the legs downwards 1.5cm (⅝in) below the central wire with pliers.

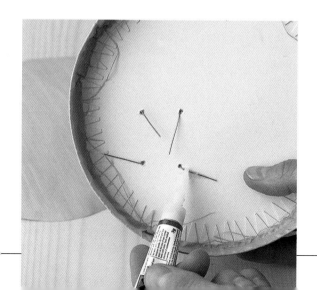

7 Thread on the remaining large beads, then two 6mm (¼in) beads, eight 3mm (⅛in) beads and four rocaille beads. Bend over the end of the wire against the last bead with the pliers. Snip off the excess wire. Arrange the dragonfly on the box lid, tipping the tail end upwards. Pierce a hole through the lid with an awl at the ends of the legs. Insert the ends of the legs through the holes and bend them backwards on the underside of the lid. Dab with super glue. Glue the lid liner inside the lid with art and hobby spray adhesive. Glue a few sequins to the lid with PVA or white glue.

patchwork
book case

THIS NOVEL BOX cleverly resembles a book – just lift the cover to reveal the storage space inside. The white textured paper, applied to the sides of the book, suggests the pages of the book. The 'book covers' are faced with silk dupion, and the 'front cover' is further embellished with a patchwork pattern outlined in sequins. A simple yet sophisticated motif formed from flower-shaped sequins is applied to the centre.

Surprise and delight family or friends with a gift of this handsome handcrafted book case, which can be filled with a set of stylish stationery. Choose a design that coordinates with the case, for added colour and impact.

patchwork
book case

you will need

mounting board

silk dupion fabric in three
colours

pair of fabric scissors

textured white paper

gummed paper tape

white acrylic paint (optional)

1m (1yd) sequin string in
two colours

2 flower-shaped sequins

variation

⤷ *Cover the book
case with imitation
leather, to resemble
a classic tome.*

1 Using a craft knife and
metal ruler, and resting on a
cutting mat, cut two rectangles
23 × 18cm (9 × 7in) for the
front and back and a strip
23 × 3.5cm (9 × 1⅜in) for the
'spine' from mounting board.
Cut a rectangle of fabric
44 × 27cm (17⅜ × 10⅝in).
Spray the wrong side of the
board pieces with spray
adhesive and stick them to
the fabric 2cm (¾in) inside
the raw edges with the spine
between the front and back.

2 Glue the corners of the
fabric over the boards, then
stick the edges of the fabric
over the boards with PVA
or white glue.

3 Cut a 21.5 × 20cm
(8⅜ × 8in) rectangle of
textured white paper. Stick
to the underside of the
front 8mm (⁵⁄₁₆in) inside
the outer edges and
extending onto the spine.

4 Refer to the diagram on page 108 to cut a box from mounting board. Score along the broken lines with a craft knife. Fold the sides upwards along the broken lines, butting the short edges together. Stick together with gummed paper tape. If the tape is likely to show through the white paper, paint the tape white.

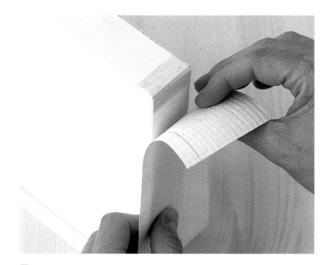

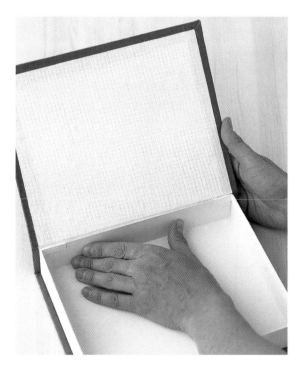

5 Cut a strip of textured white paper 59.5 × 7cm (23½ × 2¾in). Lightly draw a pencil line on the wrong side 1cm (⅜in) below the upper long edge. Spray the wrong side of the paper with spray adhesive. Stick the paper to both short and one long side of the box, with 1cm (⅜in) extending above the upper edge, and sticking the ends of the paper onto the remaining long side of the box, using the pencil line as a guide. Snip to the corners and stick the upper and lower edges inside and under the box.

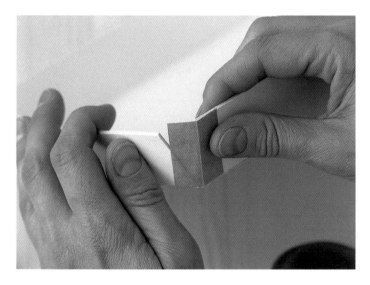

6 Spread PVA or white glue onto both the underside and the uncovered side of the box. Place the box on the back 'cover', holding the spine at right angles to the back and with the back 'cover' extending evenly around the covered edges of the box. Press the spine to the side of the box. Set aside while the glue dries.

7 Cut three rectangles 7.5 × 5.8cm (3 × 2¼in) from each of the two remaining fabrics. Spray the wrong side with art and hobby spray adhesive. Stick the pieces onto the lid, forming the patchwork design. Use PVA or white glue to stick the strings of sequins along the raw edges, gluing under the ends of the strings to start and finish to prevent the sequins from falling off. Glue two flower-shaped sequins, one on top of the other, in the middle of the centre patch.

opulent ribbon
gift boxes

LUXURIOUS RIBBONS are quite

irresistible, and a few offcuts can turn

a plain box into something very special.

Here, an inexpensive ready-made gold

heart-shaped box is decked with

ribbons, braid, sequins and lace in rich,

coordinating shades of russet and gold.

The box is also given a soft, velvet lining

edged with ribbon as a sumptuous

finishing touch.

The whole extravagant ensemble

makes the perfect package for a

romantic gift, such as your partner's

favourite indulgent confectionery, or

a superior receptacle for a precious

jewellery set.

opulent ribbon
gift boxes

you will need

selection of ribbons,
including velvet

braid, lace and string
of sequins

gold heart-shaped
gift box with lid

tiny beads

fine sewing needle

sewing thread

pair of fabric scissors

velvet

thin card

gold paint (optional)

1 Arrange lengths of ribbon,
braid and lace and a string
of sequins on the box lid.
Sew a line of tiny beads to
a length of velvet ribbon,
catching them in place
with a running stitch. Use
all-purpose household glue
to stick all the lengths in
position, sticking the ends
onto the sides of the lid.

2 Use all-purpose
household glue to stick
a length of velvet ribbon
to the sides of the lid,
starting just beyond the
inner corner of the box
and covering the raw ends
of the ribbon, braid, etc.
Trim the excess ribbon
at the inner corner.

3 Put the lid on the box
and arrange lengths of ribbon,
braid and a string of sequins
on the side of the box. Stick
in place with all-purpose
household glue, starting just
beyond the inner corner
of the box. Trim the excess
ribbon, braid and sequin
string at the inner corner.

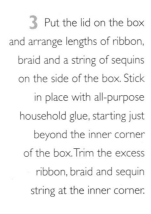

4 To line the sides inside the box, cut a strip of velvet the height of the box by its circumference plus 2.5cm (1in). Glue under 1.5cm (⅝in) at one end. Spray the back of the strip with art and hobby spray adhesive and stick the strip inside the box 1.2cm (½in) below the upper edge. Snip to the inner corner so that the velvet lays flat on the base.

5 Draw around the box base twice onto thin card. Fit one heart inside the lid. Trim 6mm (¼in) from the edges of the other and fit into the box base with at least a 1.5mm (¹⁄₁₆in) gap around the edges; trim if necessary. Stick the card hearts to the reverse of a piece of velvet with the spray adhesive. Cut out, adding a 1.5cm (⅝in) allowance. Snip to the corners and curves, then glue the raw edges to the card undersides.

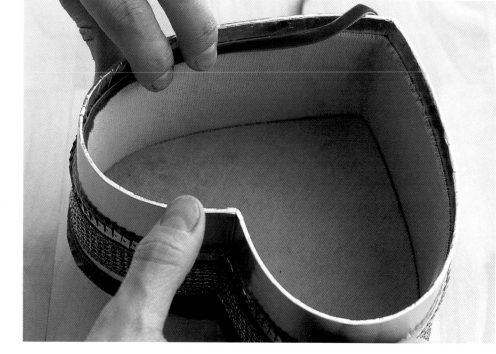

6 Paint the inside of the lid rim gold if bare card is visible. Leave to dry. Glue the covered hearts inside the lid and box with all-purpose household glue, then glue a length of narrow velvet ribbon to cover the upper raw edges of the velvet lining inside the box.

indian lotus
hat box

ALTHOUGH THERE IS HUGE CHOICE

of exciting ready-made paint stamps to

choose from nowadays, it is great fun

to create your own. They are simple to

make from fine Neoprene foam, available

from art and craft stores or suppliers,

which is very lightweight and can be cut

with scissors or a craft knife.

Here, a large hat box is covered

with shot cotton that has been stamped

with luscious Indian lotus designs. The

stamped designs are highlighted with

relief paint pens – use only those that

are suitable for fabric – and lustrous

cabochon jewellery stones, which are

simply glued onto the fabric .

indian lotus
hat box

you will need

oval or round hat box

wallpaper

neoprene foam

corrugated card

lilac shot cotton fabric

dressmaking pins

flat paintbrush

dark blue and lilac fabric paints

iron

gold and white fabric relief paint pens

medium-weight iron-on interfacing

2cm (¾in) wide lilac ribbon

cabochon jewellery stones

1 Draw around the base of the box on the wrong side of the wallpaper, adding a 1cm (⅜in) allowance to the circumference, and cut out. Spray the wrong side with art and hobby spray adhesive and stick centrally onto the inside base of the box. Smooth outwards from the centre and snip the outer edges so that the paper lays flat onto the sides of the box. Line the lid in the same way.

2 Cut a strip of wallpaper measuring the circumference of the box plus 1.5cm (⅝in) by the inside height of the box less 6mm (¼in). Spray the wrong side with the spray adhesive. Stick the strip inside the box 6mm (¼in) below the upper edges, overlapping the ends.

3 Trace the templates on page 108 onto tracing paper and cut them out using a craft knife and resting on a cutting mat. Draw around the templates with a pen onto Neoprene foam and cut them out. Stick the motifs onto corrugated card using all-purpose household glue. Cut out the card, leaving a 6mm (¼in) margin around each motif.

tip

Stamp the fabric before covering the box so that any stamping mishaps can be reworked.

4 Mark out the outline of the lid on the fabric with pins. Using a flat paintbrush, paint the lotus flower stamp with dark blue fabric paint. Press the stamp firmly onto the centre of the lid fabric, then lift it off. Mix dark blue and lilac fabric paint together. Paint the large leaf stamp. Stamp the lid fabric around the lotus flower at random with the large leaf stamp. Leave to dry thoroughly, then cut out the lid adding 1.5cm (⅝in) to the circumference.

5 Measure the circumference and height of the lid rim and the box and mark out a strip for each to size on the fabric with pins. Using the dark blue and lilac mixed fabric paint, stamp the small leaf at equal intervals centrally along the lid rim strip. Using the dark blue fabric paint, stamp the lotus bud at equal intervals centrally along the box strip. Leave the paint to dry. Cut out the pieces adding 1.5cm (⅝in) to all the edges. Press the fabric on the wrong side to fix the paint following the manufacturer's instructions.

6 Decorate the designs with relief paint pens, then set the pieces aside to dry. Cover the box and lid with the fabric pieces, referring to the techniques on pages 15 and 17. Glue lilac ribbon along the raw edges of the fabric inside the box.

7 Stick jewellery stones to the lid and box with all-purpose household glue.

variation

The papyrus was an important symbol of Ancient Egypt. The stylized papyrus templates on page 109 would be stunning worked in gold on a cream-covered hat box. Instead of outlining with relief paint, work single stitches on the papyrus with embroidery thread.

floral organza
wedding box

ALTHOUGH FLAMBOYANT IN STYLE,

this richly decorated box is quick to create

and is an excellent way of embellishing a

plain ready-made gift box.

Delicate silk flowers, sequins and lace

flowers are secured in place, protected

and enhanced by a layer of fine organza.

This sumptuous box is guaranteed to

make a memorable contribution to the

big occasion, either as a glamorous gift

box or as a special custodian of all those

precious mementos of the event, to be

kept and cherished for years to come. To

make the box especially poignant, glue

on pressed flowers from the wedding

bouquet and cover it with fabric used for

the bridal veil.

floral organza
wedding box

1 Using a craft knife and resting on a cutting mat, cut a square of giftwrap 1cm (⅜in) larger on all sides than the inside base of the box. Spray the wrong side with art and hobby spray adhesive and stick centrally onto the inside base of the box. Snip to the corners and press the paper neatly along the edges and onto the inner sides.

you will need

square pink box with lid

pink giftwrap

white and pink silk flowers

flower edging lace

round silver sequins

flower-shaped sequins

pink organza

iron

6mm (¼in) wide cream velvet ribbon

pink velvet ribbon, the width of the lid rim

2 Cut two strips of giftwrap measuring half the circumference of the box plus 1.5cm (⅝in) by the inside height of the box. Spray the wrong side with the spray adhesive. Stick the strips inside the box, matching the upper edges and overlapping the ends. Line the lid with giftwrap in the same way.

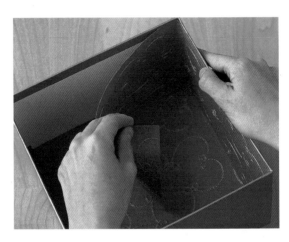

3 Carefully pull the silk flower heads off the stalks and discard the plastic centres. Cut the length of edging lace into individual flowers.

variations

> Apply shell- or leaf-shaped sequins to a tiny ring box before covering it with organza that is woven with shimmering metallic threads.

4 Glue the white flower heads and lace flowers at random to the lid using all-purpose household glue, applying it to the centre of the flower only. Glue a round sequin to the centre of each silk flower head. Glue flower-shaped sequins to the lid between the silk and lace flowers. Place the lid on the box. Glue the flowers and sequins to the sides of the box below the level of the lid in the same way.

5 Cut a square of organza 2cm (¾in) larger on all sides than the lid. Place the organza centrally on the lid. Glue the raw edges to the rim, folding under the fullness at the corners. If the rim is narrow, trim the organza so that it does not hang below the lid.

7 Glue cream velvet ribbon over the organza raw edge inside the box. Glue pink velvet ribbon to the rim of the lid. Glue pink flower heads to the rim with flower-shaped sequins between them. Cut a square of giftwrap 6mm (¼in) smaller on all edges than the box base. Stick to the underside of the base with art and hobby spray adhesive.

6 Cut a strip of organza measuring the circumference of the box plus 3cm (1¼in) by the height of the box plus 4cm (1½in). Press under 1.5cm (⅝in) at one end of the strip. Wrap the strip centrally around the box sides, overlapping the raw end with the pressed end. Glue in place. Glue the excess fabric at the upper edges inside the box and at the lower edges under the box, folding under the fullness at the lower corners.

swedish felt
sewing box

THIS GRAPHIC DESIGN, worked in white felt onto bright red fabric, is typical of traditional Swedish patterns, and is similar to the floral images customarily featured in Scandinavian cross stitch designs. The motifs are applied with bonding web, which is an iron-on backing used to fuse layers of fabric together. The box is padded and lined with cheery red gingham.

The extra padding in the lid can be employed as a pincushion, making the box an ideal container for needlework accessories, being both attractive and functional. A ribbon-and-button trimming on the lid also echoes the sewing theme.

swedish felt
sewing box

you will need

straight-sided box, at least 15cm (6in) wide, with slip-over lid

red fabric

pair of fabric scissors

fabric glue

bonding web

iron

20cm (8in) of 90cm (36in) wide white felt

pinking shears

white petersham ribbon

4 heart-shaped mother-of-pearl buttons

8 round mother-of-pearl buttons

thin card

55g (2oz) and 225g (8oz) wadding

red and white gingham fabric

1 Cover the box and lid with red fabric, referring to the techniques on pages 15–6. Trace the template on page 109 five times onto the paper backing of the bonding web. Roughly cut around the motifs, then iron each onto white felt following the manufacturer's instructions.

2 Cut along the outer square of each motif with pinking shears. Use a small, pointed, sharp pair of scissors to carefully cut away the cutouts. Peel off the paper backing. Place the lid on the box and arrange a motif centrally on the lid. Press in place with the iron to fuse the motif in place. Position and fuse a motif to each side of the box.

3 Use fabric glue to stick a length of white petersham ribbon to the rim of the lid. Use all-purpose household glue to stick one heart-shaped and two round mother-of-pearl buttons onto each side of the rim on the ribbon.

A strip of thin card is useful for spreading the glue evenly onto the back of the ribbon in Step 3 and onto the side edges of the gingham in Step 6.

4 Cut a square or rectangle of card to fit inside each side of the box, the base and underside of the lid, with a 1.5mm (1/16in) gap around the edges and a 6mm (1/4in) gap at the upper edge of the box; trim to fit if necessary. Cut four box sides and a base from 55g (2oz) wadding and a lid underside from 225g (8oz) wadding. Glue to the card pieces with fabric glue.

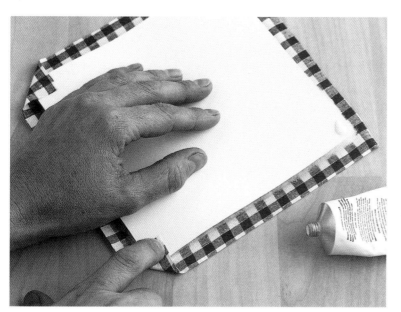

5 Cut four box sides, a base and a lid underside from gingham, adding 1.2cm (1/2in) to each edge. Place the wadding centrally face down onto the wrong side of the gingham. Lift the corners of the gingham over the card and stick in place with fabric glue.

6 Stick the side edges of the gingham smoothly over the edges of the card with fabric glue. Stick the base then the sides inside the box and the lid underside inside the lid with fabric glue.

You can use woven fabric in place of felt, since the bonding web prevents the cut edges from fraying. The fluid lines of Art Nouveau and Celtic designs would look sumptuous cut from velvet and applied to a silk-covered box (see page 109 for an Art Nouveau template). Alternatively, fuse a design cut from printed fabric to a box. A graphic motif from a nursery fabric set on a denim-covered box would delight a child.

pleated silk
casket

THIS CONTEMPORARY-STYLE pleated

fabric-covered box is worked in two

contrasting shades of vibrant silk dupion.

This fabric is particularly suitable since it

is available in many sumptuous colours

and holds the pleats well. Any light- to

medium-weight natural fabric would

work, but avoid purely synthetic fabrics

which won't hold the pleats crisply. The

pleated silk is then highlighted with

random cross stitches. An elegant

sculptural handle, shaped from thin card

and secured in place with a brass paper

fastener, adds the finishing touch.

Use the box to store cosmetics – the

shallowness of the box facilitates sorting

through the contents to coordinate shades.

pleated silk
casket

you will need

thin card

40cm (½yd) of 90cm
(36in) wide red and
purple silk dupion

iron

air-erasable pen or tailor's chalk

sewing needle and thread

purple stranded cotton
embroidery thread

crewel embroidery needle

60cm (⅔yd) of 1.5cm (⅝in)
wide purple ribbon

corrugated card

awl

brass paper fastener

super glue

2 weighty items, e.g. small,
heavy books

1 Use the templates and diagram on page 110 to cut a base and side panel from thin card. Score along the lines of the side panel and bend the panel backwards along the scored lines. Apply double-sided tape to the lower tabs on the wrong side and to the end tab on the right side. Snip the lower edge to the scored line at 6mm (¼in) intervals. Peel off the backing. Matching the vertical folds to the points of the base, wrap the panel around the base, sticking the lower tabs under the base. Stick the end tab under the opposite end of the panel.

2 Cut a strip of red silk to line the box 56 × 8cm (22 × 3¼in). Press under 1.5cm (⅝in) at one end and stick in place with PVA or white glue. Spray the wrong side with art and hobby spray adhesive and stick inside the box 6mm (¼in) below the upper edge with the lower edge of the fabric extending onto the base. Overlap the raw end with the pressed end. Snip the fabric to the corners and at the curves of the base so that it lays flat.

3 Cut a rectangle of red silk 57 × 17.5cm (22¼ × 6¾in). With an air-erasable pen or tailor's chalk, draw eight lines on the silk parallel with the long edges at 1.5cm (⅝in) intervals, starting 3cm (1¼in) inside the upper and lower edges. To pleat, bring the first (top) line to the second line, the third line to the forth line and so on, making four pleats. Press in place.

4 Sew a line of tacking stitches 6mm (¼in) in along the short edges of the fabric. Thread a crewel embroidery needle with four strands of purple stranded cotton embroidery thread. Work cross stitches at random on the pleats, singly and in pairs. Follow the technique on page 15 to cover the box with the pleated fabric. Stick a length of ribbon over the raw edges inside the box using PVA or white glue.

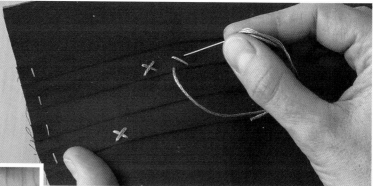

5 Use the template on page 110 to cut a base liner from thin card. Cut a lid and lid liner from corrugated card. From red silk, cut a base liner adding 1.5cm (⅝in) to the circumference. From purple silk, cut a lid adding 2.5cm (1in) to the circumference and a lid liner adding 2cm (¾in) to the circumference. Stick the card pieces centrally onto the fabric using art and hobby spray adhesive. Snip the fabric to 2mm (¹⁄₁₆in) from the base liner and 1cm (⅜in) from the lid and lid liner. Glue to the wrong side of the card, starting at the corners, using PVA or white glue, and stick the base liner inside the box.

6 Use the template on page 110 to cut one handle from both the red and purple silk and one from thin card, cutting along the relevant cutting lines. Press under 1cm (⅜in) on the straight edges of the silk fabric handles. With right sides facing, stitch the handles together taking a 1cm (⅜in) seam allowance, leaving the pressed edge open. Snip the seam allowance at the corners and curves. Turn right side out and press.

7 Pull the card handle between your fingers to curve it, then insert into the fabric sleeve. Slipstitch the pressed edges together. Pierce a hole through the dots on the handle and lid with an awl. Lap the narrow end of the handle over the wide end, matching the holes. Insert the prongs of a brass paper fastener through the holes from the inside of the handle. Insert the prongs through the hole on the lid and splay them open on the wrong side. Stick the prongs in place with super glue. Stick the lid liner centrally under the lid with super glue. Place weights on the lid, one each side of the handle, while the glue dries.

templates

Templates need to be enlarged as stated

embossed metal canister • p20

Enlarge templates by 200%

embossed metal canister design variation

italian-wrap hanging boxes • p32

Enlarge templates by 200%

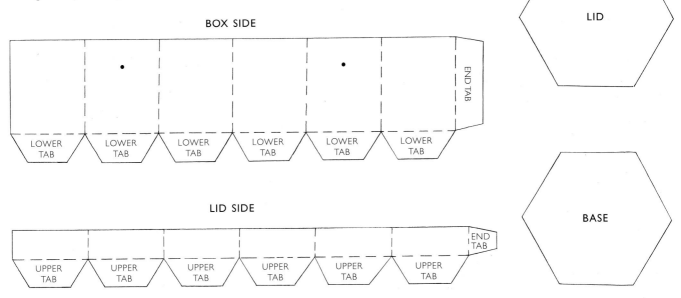

BOX SIDE

END TAB

LOWER TAB · LOWER TAB · LOWER TAB · LOWER TAB · LOWER TAB · LOWER TAB

LID

LID SIDE

END TAB

UPPER TAB · UPPER TAB · UPPER TAB · UPPER TAB · UPPER TAB · UPPER TAB

BASE

paper marquetry chess box • p28

Enlarge templates by 200%

TOP OF LID

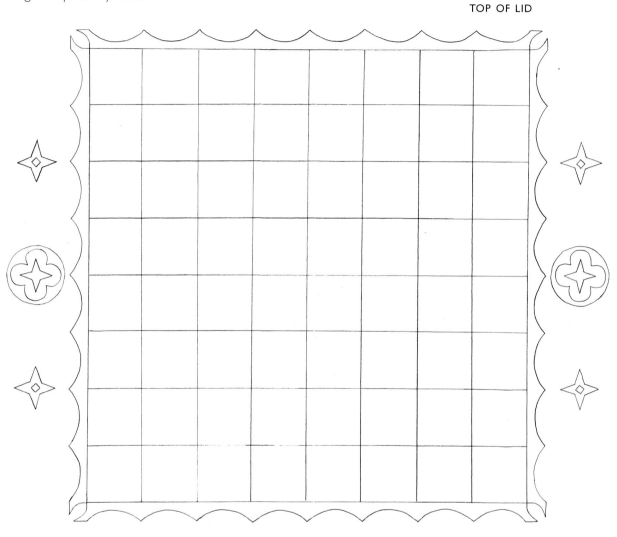

BOX SIDE

BOX SIDE

SIDE OF LID

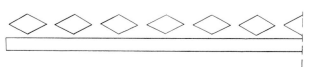

terracotta and lichen casket • p66

Enlarge template by 200%

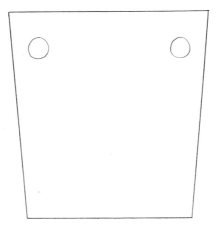

SIDE PANEL

oriental etched pot • p36

Use actual size shown

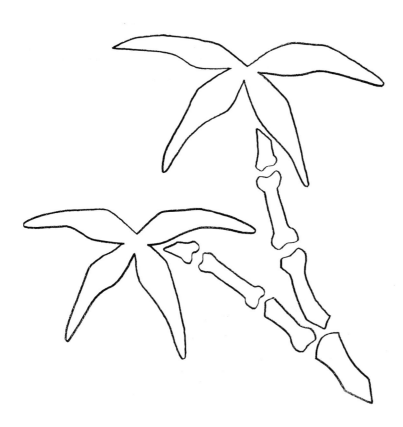

oriental etched pot
design variation

classical mosaic chest ● p58

Enlarge templates by 200%

classical mosaic chest design variation

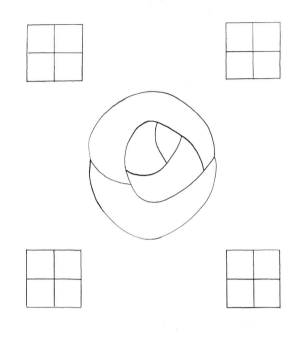

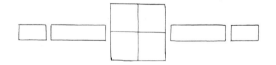

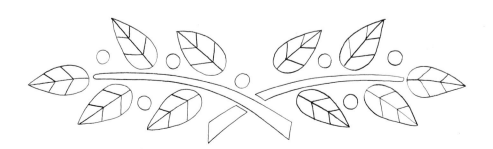

beaded dragonfly
jewellery box • p76

Enlarge template by 150%

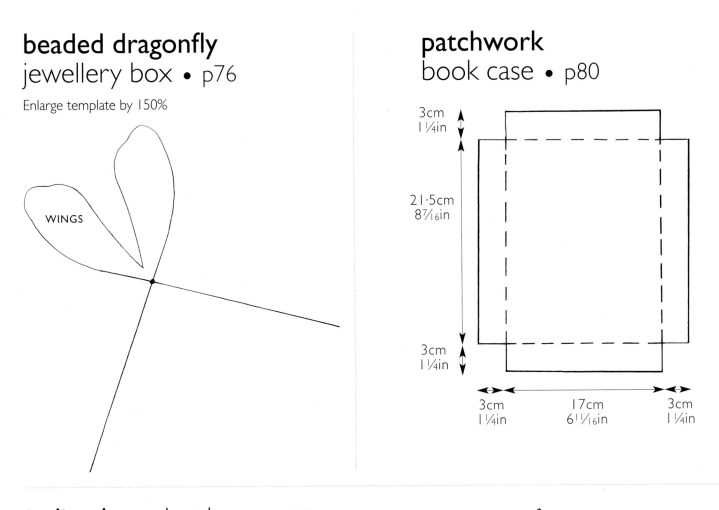

WINGS

patchwork
book case • p80

3cm
1¼in

21·5cm
8⁷⁄₁₆in

3cm
1¼in

3cm
1¼in

17cm
6¹¹⁄₁₆in

3cm
1¼in

indian lotus hat box • p88

Use actual size shown

LARGE LEAF

SMALL
LEAF

LOTUS BUD

LOTUS FLOWER

swedish felt sewing box • p96

Enlarge templates by 150%

swedish felt sewing box
design variation

indian lotus hat box
design variation

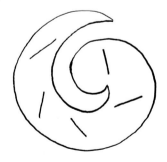

pleated silk casket • p100

Enlarge template by 125%

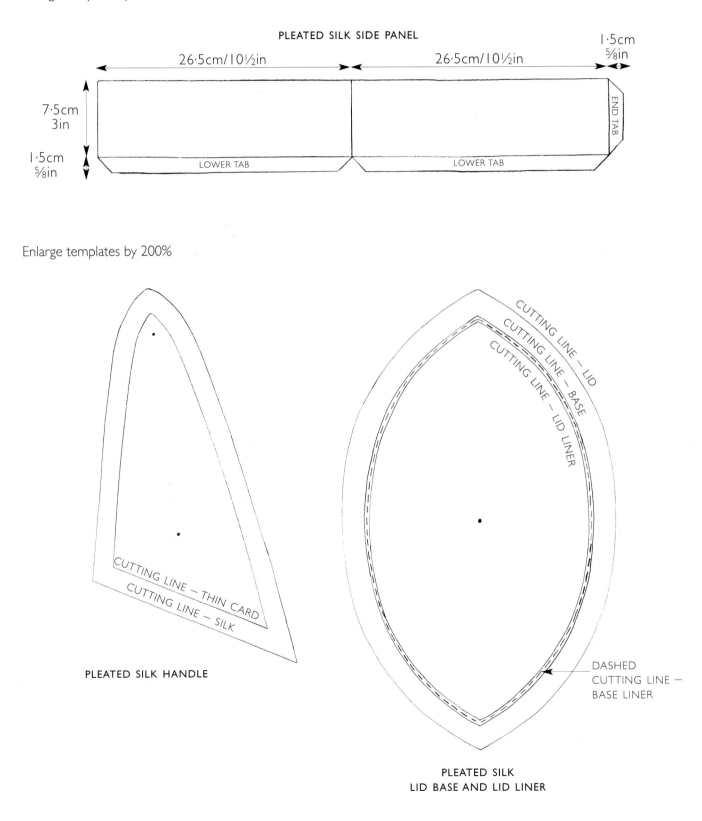

PLEATED SILK SIDE PANEL

26·5cm/10½in

26·5cm/10½in

1·5cm
⅝in

7·5cm
3in

END TAB

1·5cm
⅝in

LOWER TAB

LOWER TAB

Enlarge templates by 200%

CUTTING LINE – THIN CARD
CUTTING LINE – SILK

PLEATED SILK HANDLE

CUTTING LINE – LID
CUTTING LINE – BASE
CUTTING LINE – LID LINER

DASHED
CUTTING LINE –
BASE LINER

PLEATED SILK
LID BASE AND LID LINER

making a square or rectangular box and lid • p13

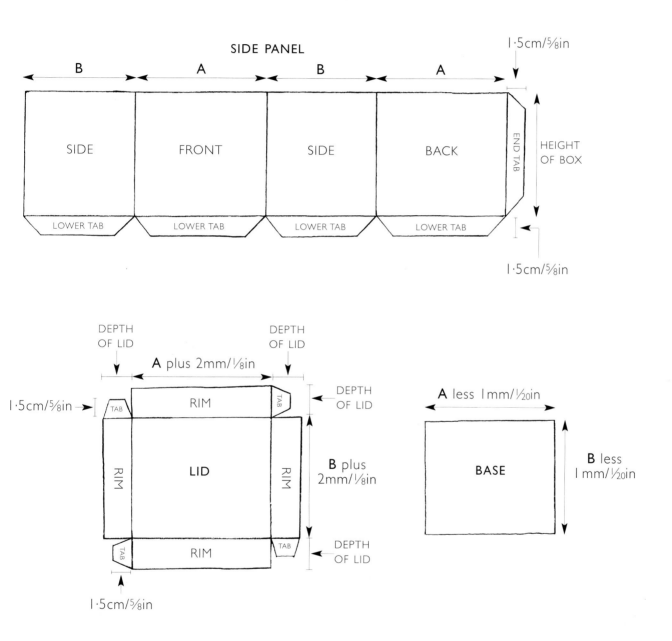

SIDE PANEL

1·5cm/⅝in

B   A   B   A

SIDE   FRONT   SIDE   BACK

END TAB

HEIGHT OF BOX

LOWER TAB   LOWER TAB   LOWER TAB   LOWER TAB

1·5cm/⅝in

DEPTH OF LID   DEPTH OF LID

A plus 2mm/⅛in

1·5cm/⅝in

TAB   RIM   TAB

RIM   LID   RIM

DEPTH OF LID

B plus 2mm/⅛in

TAB   RIM   TAB

DEPTH OF LID

1·5cm/⅝in

A less 1mm/¹⁄₂₀in

BASE

B less 1mm/¹⁄₂₀in

index

suppliers

UK
3M UK plc
3M House
PO Box 1
Market Place
Bracknell
Berkshire RG12 1JU
tel: 01344 858000
website: www.mmm.com/uk
(spray adhesives; available from art
and craft shops and suppliers –
contact for your nearest stockist)

Celestial
162 Archway Road
London N6 5BB
tel: 020 8341 2788
(ribbons, trimmings and buttons)

Fred Aldous
37 Lever Street
Manchester M1 1LW
tel: 0161 2362477
website: www.fredaldous.co.uk
(craft materials by mail order)

Harvey Baker Design Ltd
Unit 5
Rodgers Industrial Estate
Yalberton Road
Paignton
Devon TQ4 7PJ
tel: 01803 521515
website: www.harvey-baker-design.co.uk
(wooden box 'blanks' by mail order)

Home Crafts Direct
PO Box 38
Leicester LE1 9BU
tel: 0845 4584561
website: www.homecrafts.co.uk
(craft materials by mail order)
Perivale-Gütermann Ltd

Bullsbrook Road
Hayes
Middlesex UB4 0JR
tel: 020 8589 1600
website: www.guetermann.com
(beads and sequins; available at
haberdashery shops and departments –
contact for your nearest stockist)

Scumble Goosie
Lewiston Mill
Toads More Road
Stroud
Gloucestershire GL5 2TB
tel: 01453 731305
website: www.scumblegoosie.com
(wooden box 'blanks' by mail order)

US
Beadworks
290 Thayer Street
Providence, RI 02906
tel: (401) 861-4540
(beads and findings)

Ribbons
C.M. Offray & Son, Inc.
360 Route 24
Chester, NJ 07930
tel: (800) 551-LION
website: www.offray.com
(decorative ribbons)

Viking Woodcrafts, Inc.
1317 8th Street SE
Waseca, MN 56093
tel: 800-328-0116
fax: 507-835-3895
website: vikingwoodcrafts.com
(wooden box 'blanks')

ACKNOWLEDGMENTS
Special thanks to Fiona Eaton, Jennifer Proverbs and Ali Myer
at David & Charles, to Jo Richardson for her attention to
detail and Ginette Chapman for the beautiful photography.